Thou

Stanley Drake

Though you Die

Death and Life beyond Death

Floris Books

This edition revised by Peter van Breda

First published in 1962
Fourth edition 2002
© The Christian Community, 1962, 2002

British Library Cataloguing in Publication Data

Drake, Stanley, *1906–1986*
Though you die: death and life beyond death.—4th ed.
1. Death — Philosophical perspectives
I. Title
128.'5

ISBN 0-86315-369-0

Printed in Europe

Contents

Acknowledgments

I gratefully acknowledge the permissions granted by publishers and copyright holders for the use of the following extracts and quotations:

From Charles Lindbergh's *The Spirit of St. Louis,* John Murray Publishers; from Frank Smythe's *The Spirit of the Hills,* the Viscountess Malden and Hodder and Stoughton; from John Masefield's poem: *A Creed,* the Society of Authors and Dr John Masefield,

Unless otherwise noted, all quotations from the Bible are from the Revised Standard Version.

Foreword

If death is nothing but extermination, we surely have no difficulty in understanding the point of view of those who say, 'Eat, drink and be merry, for tomorrow we may die.' The nihilistic attitude so common in our times is reinforced by the thought that our Earth may be made uninhabitable by human activities within a generation or two. But if, in contrast, death can be seen as the doorway to a new sphere of existence, vastly different and strange by our earthly standards, yet a state in which our 'self' continues to exist and evolve, then the bleak materialism of modern culture can at least be shot through with some rays of light.

Having read so far, the reader may well say, 'Yes, I know that, but it: doesn't help me much.' True. There is a great need therefore to bring our thinking about death on to a more realistic level and to penetrate, as far as we can, into a knowledge of the facts. That is what in a modest way this book sets out to do. There is more that is knowable about death than many people think. There are experiences of the brink of death which are not much spoken about. There are sources of knowledge which are not very widely known, and, above all, there is the central Christian mystery of Christ's overcoming of death, the full significance of which has certainly not yet been grasped by human thinking and which will only reveal itself as that thinking becomes increasingly more spiritual.

The approach attempted here to this huge subject is not that of the scientist, nor is it merely theological. Death is seen as a human problem, a question for every man and woman. Therefore we begin from ordinary human experience. But when we come to the frontier zone of life and death, the experience begins to become extraordinary because a different order of existence now impinges on the accustomed one. The thoughts we shall have to think will have to be of a correspondingly different order. Here I must make it clear that the writing of this book would have been unthinkable without a number of years' study of the writings of Rudolf Steiner and without the experience on the sacramental and pastoral level which my work as a priest in The Christian Community has brought me.

Stanley Drake

Death being the way and condition of life; we cannot love to live if we cannot bear to die. I have often wondered at the unaccountableness of man in this among other things; that though he loves changes so well, he should care so little to hear or think of his last, great and best change too, if he pleases. The truest end of Life is to know the Life that never ends. He that lives to live ever never fears dying. Nor can the means be terrible to him that heartily believes the end. For though Death be a dark passage, it leads to Immortality, and that's recompense enough for suffering of it.

William Penn

1 The Fear of Death

We live in a pessimistic age and increasingly the question is asked as to the meaning of our existence. Is all we can expect of our life the helpless childhood phase, misunderstood and lonely teenager years, over-burdened adulthood, then the neglect and weariness of old age? Many people struggle for years to find meaningful work and to afford a suitable roof over their heads, and end up wondering why they were ever born. Is there no more to our sojourn here on Earth than suffering and emptiness of purpose and then the finality of death?

Small wonder, then, that even in our modern uninhibited culture, to discuss frankly the fact and experience of death is something which is still 'not done.' Convention allows the most intense discussion of politics, sport, and even religion in some circumstances, but the average person shies off talking about death. It is not good form. If we speak about someone who has died, we refer mainly to what that person was in their life, what their qualities were (with a tendency to forget their less worthy ones), and what consequences their death has had for the family. We do not discuss what has been happening to them since they died! Indeed, most people would say it is ridiculous to do so, for how can we know anything about it?

That may sound very reasonable, yet behind it lurks an uneasiness, an uncomfortable fear. We push away the painful subject, just as we mostly put off going to the dentist until sheer pain and discomfort make us face it. Yet why should we adopt this ostrich-like attitude to the one great certainty of our existence on the Earth, to the one great experience which everyone must have sooner or later? Is it not something which one might expect to be of the greatest interest to everyone? Would it not be worth while to find out as much as we can about it in order that we may think of death a little less as a leap into the unknown? To do this does not mean that we are morbid or gloomy people; it is a sign that we take an interest in the deeper realities of life.

We are afraid when we think of death, partly because we associate so much unpleasantness with dying. We think of the many horrible forms of death of which we have heard: people trapped in burning buildings, or in the wreckage of a train crash, or the prolonged agony of a painful illness. It is natural and human to shrink from pain and suffering. But this is distinct from the experience of death itself, that change by which 'we' separate from our body, leaving it to be dissolved into the elements which have composed it. This too calls up in us a very deep-rooted, instinctive feeling of fear. We find it hard to think of ourselves existing apart from our physical body, for it is just that which provides the basis for our normal waking consciousness, and we do not like losing consciousness, except through the natural process of sleep.

To die is so final, so irrevocable, that we do not like to contemplate the possibility, and here lies a positive aspect of the fear of death: it keeps us alive! Without this the number of deaths on the road would be still greater than it already, tragically, is. That instinctive fear-reaction to the sight of an oncoming vehicle rushing straight at you stimulates you to get out of the way more quickly or to make a frantic effort to avert tragedy. The temptation to commit suicide would also be greater if the element of fear did not hold many people back from it.

We find a deeper reflection on attitudes to death and

dying in the work of Dr Elisabeth Kübler-Ross who was born in Switzerland and has worked for many years in America. In her lifetime she has won renown for her seminars with medical students, doctors, nurses and social workers. The point she makes is that while the technical training of students in the physiological aspects of death has advanced, the study of human relationships of doctors and nurses to terminally ill patients is neglected, so that even these professionals may be embarrassed by situations they do not know how to deal with though they meet them almost daily.

The taboo against talking about death or dying still persists strongly and requires a conscious effort to overcome it. Yet these seminars have shown that in very many cases the terminally ill patient, the person who knows that he or she is dying, is relieved to find someone — doctor, nurse or chaplain — who is willing to talk realistically and not in platitudes about death and what follows. Dr Ross divides the phases through which such a patient goes into five steps: denial, anger, bargaining, depression, acceptance. Medical and other attendants have to reckon with these states and find ways of dealing with them, which is often far from easy.

'To work with the dying patient requires a certain maturity which only comes from experience. We have to take a good look at our own attitude toward death and dying before we can sit quietly and without anxiety next to a terminally ill patient.' So Dr Ross sums up her view in her book *On Death and Dying* in which she records the transcripts of many of her seminars and conversations.

But was this fear of death always present in humankind? Or was there a point where it began? I believe there was, and that we find an indication of it in the Bible. If we are prepared to take the book of Genesis seriously as a document containing spiritual truths about the history of humanity, even if they are clothed in mythological forms, then I think we may infer from the story of the Creation and Fall of Man that this relationship to death was not originally what it is for humankind today. For Genesis says: 'And the LORD God commanded the man, saying, "You may freely eat of every tree of the garden; but of the tree of the knowledge of good and evil you shall not eat, for in the day that you eat of it you shall die".' (Gen.2:16f). Or, rendering the Hebrew more literally: *'dying thou shalt die.'* This seems to suggest that, whatever we may understand the eating of the tree of knowledge to have been, it did have as consequence that death became a darker and more incisive experience than hitherto. Or we might say that then, for the first time, Man became aware of the fact of death, which had up to then only been a kind of dream.

The problem of death is bound up with the question of the survival of consciousness — a matter we shall discuss further in later chapters. But let us first consider what it is in ordinary everyday life that gives us that sense of self to which we are accustomed, the feeling: 'Here I am, I perceive the world around me. As an individual I have a relationship to the world.' There are three things which we possess as human beings, which distinguish us from all other creatures of nature: upright posture, the power of speech, and the power of thought. These give us our humanity and our human consciousness.

The upright posture is something which gives man dignity; the human spine is meant to be vertical to the earth, and when I stand upright, I can feel myself more as an 'I' than if my body is horizontal. If I am lying down and someone comes into the room and says something which makes me angry, I feel impelled to leap to my feet, draw myself up straight and say with the full force of my personality: 'You ...!' I do not feel happy to 'take it lying down.' It is not without significance that the word 'I' is represented by a vertical stroke, or that uprightness describes an moral quality.

The power of speech is something for which we look eagerly in the development of the small child. One who is dumb is deprived, not only of the means of making their needs, wishes and opinions known to others, but also of those finer shades of human relationships which come out through the 'how' of our speaking rather than through the 'what.' If I speak, I reveal something of myself, irrespective of what I say. The power of thought, like the other two capacities, distinguishes Man from the animals. A crab does not think. The journeyings of the salmon and the migration of birds are among the wonderful achievements of nature, but one cannot imagine that the thinking of any one salmon or bird plans and carries through the whole operation. With domesticated animals, their intelligent reaction to certain sets of circumstances may give the impression to some people that they 'think,' but this in truth has nothing in common with man's power to create in thought. That we can share a thought with another person is one of the beauties of human existence, a means whereby my 'I' finds a connection to the 'I' of another.

So the consciousness of our self springs from these three qualities. But besides saying 'I,' we also say 'my.' And that means that our 'I' becomes attached to certain things which we call our possessions, and these become a support to our self-awareness. We feel ourselves more of an individual when we say: This is *my* house; this is *my* bicycle. To own a car gives a sense of power: I can travel where I will, when I will. To have a solid bank balance gives a sense of security: I know I can buy what I need. Such things are supports to our self-consciousness, and it is a great test of individuality how a person faces the loss of possessions. For those who have had to flee from their homes or who lose everything in the way of personal ownership, these supports are taken away. It was a cruelly devised technique used in the Soviet concentration camps to deprive the prisoners of all worldly possessions, and even the use of their names was withheld from them. Even now, refugees who settle in another country have to reckon with their fears and even mistrust towards those who with goodwill set out to help them.

The things we gather around us are thus a kind of projection of our 'self' on the material plane, and is not part of our instinctive fear of death a fear of the loss of just this support? Nothing of what we have goes with us through the gate of death, only what we are, what we have become in the course of our life, whether with the aid of those supports, or in spite of them, or without them. 'Lay not up for yourselves treasure upon earth,' said Christ to his disciples, for they had to acquire the other kind of treasure. They had to acquire not 'wasting assets,' but 'permanent assets' which would detain their full value beyond death. And therein lies part of the secret of overcoming at least this aspect of our fear of death: that our real self, our true 'I,' becomes so strong that it can without difficulty dispense with those earthly supports which are in fact only spiritual crutches.

It may well be asked at this point: But what is my 'real self,' my 'true I'? And how do I become aware of this self? The English writer Owen Barfield suggests that we come closer to a sense of self if we begin a process by which we identify that which we are not. Once we have identified and discarded all the trimmings and outer sheaths and masks of our personality we will become gradually conscious of our essential self.

These outer guises are many. I may walk through life here on Earth carrying in my body the genes of my forefathers, but this is not my true identity. I am not simply all that I have inherited. Likewise I am not my nationality, my culture or my language, nor even my emotions and passions. Of course all these things influence me profoundly but I know from moments of meditation or from times of religious insight that I am another. I am capable of refining and mastering those feelings and passions that well up within me and so it is with all the other sheaths that create my earthly expression. In essence I know that I am an individual intertwined and interwoven into the matrix of the whole human race. But that is not all; stirring within me is an inner knowledge that I have come from another world and that at some point I will return to it. That both you and I have an individuality destined for eternity.

Rudolf Steiner speaks of the 'I' as the core of man's being. It is not something which a human being has to produce. It is their very self.

> In his 'I' man brings together all that he experiences as a being with body and soul. Body and soul are the carriers of the ego or 'I'; in them it acts. Just as the physical body has its centre in the brain, so has the soul its centre in the ego. Man is aroused to sensations by impacts from without; feelings manifest themselves as effects of the outer world; the will relates itself to the outside world in that it realises itself in external actions. The 'I' as the peculiar and essential being of man remains quite invisible ... And this 'I' is the man himself.

That justifies him in regarding his ego as his true being.

Body and soul yield themselves up to the 'I' in order to serve it; but the 'I' yields itself up to the spirit in order that the spirit may fill it to overflowing — The 'I' lives in body and soul but the spirit lives in the 'I.' And what there is of spirit in the 'I' is eternal. *(Theosophy,* London 1970, p.35.)

For this experience of self to arise within us, we will need to practise again and again an 'active inwardness.' By this I mean prayer and contemplation, meditation and spiritual activity in a Christian sense. Also some part of our more temporal nature that so often clings to the material world must learn to die. A free space needs to be created within our souls for this true and precious self to be revealed. We are especially helped to achieve this awakening and affirmation of selfhood through a conscious relationship to the Christ, who is our brother and guide. St Paul expresses this with the words: 'For you have died and your life [that is, your true being] is hid with Christ in God.' (Col. 3:3). It is through this active inwardness and growing awareness of the presence of Christ that we find our connection to our own spirit being and with the world of spirit.

It is this world of spirit which we approach through the experience of death, and in so far as it is a world of the unknown, we may feel fear when we contemplate the possibility of entering it. But it is the theme of this book that it is not an unknowable world, that it is possible to have some advance information about its nature. But, assuming for the moment that the world beyond death is neither a complete vacuum nor blank unconsciousness, and that it is not unpopulated, then the prospect of entering a spiritual world and encountering unknown spiritual beings has naturally some thing alarming about it. One may not know how to behave, what to do! Many people feel nervous at the thought of entering a room full of complete strangers, being uncertain as to what sort of reception they will get and what may be expected of them. We all know the slight shock we get if we go into a room which we believe to be empty, and then, after a few moments, discover the presence of someone sitting silently in a corner of the room.

The Bible contains many descriptions of the appearances of angelic beings, and nearly always the first reaction is one of fear. For example St Luke tells us that the women who came to the tomb seeking Jesus were afraid when they saw the two men in shining garments, who said to them, 'Why do you seek the living among the dead?' And when the Risen Christ appeared to the disciples: 'they were startled and frightened, and supposed that they saw a spirit. And he said to them, "Why are you troubled? ... it is I myself".' (Luke 24:37f.)

It is above all our living relationship to the being of Christ that can take away from us the fear of death.

When the end of earth-life comes, let us not think that we have reached the twilight, or that for the last time the golden sky is fading in the West. Let us not think that night has come, but that a grander sunrise awaits us beyond the grave. We must meet death as we meet sleep, knowing that the morning follows the night. Thus we should enter the dawn called Death ...

Death is but the name given to the door through which we enter to reach another phase of our existence. What appears a dream between the shores of birth and death is a great reality, and though we seem to stand upon the verge of crumbling time, to love, to hope and disappear, yet it is the greatest of life's many certainties that each individual life will never die, because each one of us is part of the Divine Mind.

J.A. Findlay

If Death Sleep's brother be
And souls bereft of sense have so sweet dreams
How could I wish thus still to dream and die!

William Drummond of Hawthornden

2 Approach to Death

When we are children, the fact of death does not mean very much to us. Parents are sometimes taken aback by the matter of-fact attitude which their child displays towards the death of a well-loved relative. That Auntie has gone to be with the angels is just as objective a fact as if she had gone to live with her brother in Australia. There is no tragic feeling about it. And this is right and natural, for the child under the age of fourteen has no relationship to the sphere of death. In fairy tales heads get chopped off, people are killed and brought to life again, and many things occur which some parents consider too blood-thirsty for the children, but the children themselves are not shocked by these stories. They do not arouse in them the same emotions which the contemplation of similar events, described historically, would do for the adult. They are on a different plane.

Of course, the death of the mother of a family of young children is deeply felt, but less because the children have experienced the awe and dread of death than because of the big gap left in daily life through the loss of the mother. Yet, apart from individual variations, the general mood of childhood is sanguine, and, if sadness comes, it is soon forgotten.

It is another matter if a child receives the shock of see-ing their mother or father killed in a road accident or other disaster. That will leave a deep wound in a child's soul, the consequences of which can last a lifetime. But, apart from being thus confronted with the experience, the idea of death has little meaning for most children. When death happens, the children are most protected by the degree of calmness which the adults can maintain in their presence.

With puberty a new phase is reached. A step forward is being taken — a step deeper down into the joys and sorrows which earthly life brings. The emotions are more deeply felt and the death of a close relative or friend can cut very deeply into the soul of a young person in their teens. All the capacity for feeling and suffering is there, but without, as yet, the maturity and knowledge to balance it.

So far we have only considered the death of others. It is a further step to consider, calmly and consciously, the possibility of dying oneself There is a deep-rooted tendency in most of us instinctively to exclude ourselves when discussing death or other catastrophes that can shake the foundations of life. How often does a person, finding himself in an unexpected plight, say: 'I never thought this would happen to me!' It is a kind of self-protection, but also a self-deception that we put up a defence against what is too unpleasant. Even in war, though we know rationally and logically that there is a possibility of our being killed, we in fact assume — and perhaps have to assume — that we shall go on living.

In the first half of life we are growing down into our physical body — settling into our earthly house, we might call it. Our life begins when we take our first breath and each morning, when we wake up, we breathe in deeply. Our breathing capacity, measured quite externally by chest expansion, increases through all the years of growth. Up to about the age of thirty-five we are breathing in a little more, if anything, than we are breathing out. From the mid-thirties we begin to breathe out, and we go on breathing out until our last breath. This change from breathing in to breathing out is a gentle, imperceptible one; just as when we sit by the sea-shore watching the waves, the turn of the tide cannot actually be seen at a precise moment, though it can be calculated and we can see its effects. This gives the physiological basis for a different attitude to death.

I remember, not long after my thirty-fifth year, walking across a field amongst the Derbyshire hills and suddenly realizing: 'One day I shall leave this earth. These fields, these rocks and hills will remain, but I shall be gone. I am just as much a visitor on this earth, as I am at the moment a visitor to this countryside.' So with advancing years we begin to think differently about our relationship to life and death.

The Psalmist wrote: 'The years of our life are three-score and ten, or even by reason of strength fourscore; yet their span is but toil and trouble; they are soon gone, and we fly away.' (90:10). We are reminded here of the transitory nature of our life, that it is very short in relation to the time-scale of the divine plan, and that what we do has no very great significance spiritually. This sounds negative and depressing. Nor may we feel much encouraged by the following verse: 'Who considers the power of thy anger?' But then comes a positive thought which is very relevant to our theme: 'So teach us to number our days that we may get a heart of wisdom.' Numbering our days does not mean reckoning how much longer we may expect to live but rather that we should cultivate the memory of what we have experienced and make conscious to ourselves the significance of what we have, or have not, achieved in the successive stages of our life. Out of this systematic reflection on life can grow the wisdom of the heart.

For those who live well beyond the 'allotted span' of years much will depend on whether they have discovered this secret of living. Those years can be 'years of grace' if we have learned to look on earthly life as a great opportunity for development and advance in self-knowledge, if we have taken our destiny in hand and made something of it ourselves out of that element of freedom of which man is potentially capable only on the Earth. Our life's work is accomplished, whether well or badly. What is now our task?

If we have preserved the faculty of a clear mind, even if our body is sick, we can do much. Firstly, it is right to live in our memories of the past. They are our most treasured possession. We do the greatest service to old people by listening to their reminiscences (there is a great art in sympathetic listening!) and helping them to clarify their memories. These, as we shall see, are most important to them after death.

But now is also the time to look forward to the great adventure which lies beyond death. We are as if waiting for a ship to take us across the ocean to a new country. How long the ship will be in coming we do not know. We wait patiently near the harbour, and, having disposed of all our affairs and belongings in the country we are about to leave, focus our thoughts on the land we are bound for; or study the elements of wind and wave to which we are about to commit ourselves.

At the same time it should not be forgotten what blessings can be given by the aged who have grown old in the right way, who have made the adjustments which their advancing years demand and learned the great secret of acceptance. This principle of acceptance does not mean that we adopt a passive and spineless attitude to the facts which surround us in life — we may even take energetic steps to alter them — but, when we are faced with situations we cannot alter, which may include accidents, illness or bereavement, we do not struggle against them in futile resentment and bitterness, but seek ways and means to turn even disabilities to good account and to let sorrow be a seed-bed of wisdom. Those people who have done this, in spite of many difficulties, and made their adjustments to life, when they grow old seem to be surrounded by an atmosphere of peace. Their souls are like calm pools, reflecting the serenity of the stars.

At one time I used to visit a lady of over ninety who was entirely bedridden; her sight had failed, but her mind was clear and alert and she took an interest in news of the world outside. She had no near relatives and was first in one nursing home, then in another, and finally in the 'chronic ward' of a hospital. Her surroundings were often anything but pleasant. She could not read and had few visitors, and the days must have seemed interminable. Yet whenever I went to her, she was cheerful and extraordinarily grateful for the very little I could do for her. The atmosphere of graciousness and peace which radiated from her was a refreshment as compared with the bustle and strain of life.

There are many such souls who can give much, especially to children, who often love to be with them. There is a mysterious bond between those who are not far from the gate of birth and those who are near the gate of death.

Yet we know all too well that it is relatively few people who reach this experience of a pool of peace and calm at the end of life. They are the souls who through their basic attitude to life and their self-development have won through to it. They have learned just what life can give them and have not expected more of life than it can give.

How many others there are who reach the end of life with a vague feeling that life has somehow cheated them, that they *ought* to have had a better time of it and therefore life owes them something. These are the bitter, grumbling, crotchety old people, who are a burden to themselves and others and whose care and welfare is such a headache to relatives, who want to do the right thing for their old people but have neither the capacity nor the means for doing it. It is a labour of sheer love and self-sacrifice to give them what they need, not just for their bodies but especially for their souls, that they may be prepared for their crossing into another world which is so different.

Yet the immediate approach to death itself is only in rare cases a peaceful decline of the powers of our physical body and then a final outbreathing. In the great majority of cases (excluding for the moment accidents and other violent forms of death) there is some kind of illness leading up to it, short or long, acute or chronic. In the course of that illness there will come a point where the doctor comes to the opinion that there is danger of death. He may hint as much to the relatives, who then usually do their best to keep the fact from the patient. This they do partly from an unwillingness to admit to their own consciousness the thought that the one they love must go from them, partly from a sense of helplessness and embarrassment. How should one speak to a person who is dying?

It is important to take the situation in hand from the psychological and spiritual angle, just when attention is so often focused almost exclusively on physical symptoms. For sooner or later, according to the nature of the illness and the constitution of the person, comes the time when he or she knows that there is no recovery possible, that the earthly destiny is reaching its end. Then there should be no pretence, but a realistic making ready for the journey in which the sick physical body will have no part.

Here is the point where, if not already a regular visitor, as they should be in any serious illness, a minister or priest should be sent for, because this preparing of the soul for its future state is quite specifically their task. (For the practical details of this preparation, see Chapter 5.)

But how different can the approach to death be! How can it look to those who are not old or sick, but who are in the midst of healthy, vigorous life. Mostly such people do not think about it much, but those who in their pursuits and occupations run greater risk of accidental death may reflect on it.

Let one who as a mountaineer has seen catastrophe to his fellows and been near it himself give his view. The mountaineer and author Frank Smythe evolved out of his experience 'in high places' a view of life and death through which the bracing winds of the mountain-top blow refreshingly:

> The possibility of being gassed or bombed or shot appals me, not because I die as a result of the process, but because it is such an artificial and ridiculous ending. The possibility of falling from a mountain or dying in a storm does not appal me, because it is a natural ending in which I have a personal interest and responsibility. To me death, when it is associated with a manufactured or mechanical element, is more terrible than when it is associated with a pristine natural element. Possibly this is because we are put into the world by natural means and are presumed to leave it by natural means, so that any action of ours which sets that Divine intention or pre-supposition by the ears is contrary to the rhythmic evolution of our progress.

I have bivouacked with a man who told me that he believes that at death consciousness as well as life ceases to exist. His view was that everything resulted from chance. When I saw Nature in all her splendour — the mountains above us, the star-strewn heaven above the mountains — I reflected, what a chance!

In my own case, my instinctive convictions favour survival. These may ... be due to a funda-mental instinct which tells me that only an all-see-ing Providence, a Directive Power, could have evolved a universe which my mountaineering friend, already mentioned, prefers to ascribe to mere chance. I look forward, therefore, to death with interest, and wish at the same time that I could look backward beyond birth, if only to sat-isfy an interest in reincarnation which has always seemed to me a simple explanation, in part at least, of evolution ...

There is no doubt that to most people an ideal death is one that strikes instantaneously and with-out warning, but, failing that, there are a number of easy deaths, and death by falling on a mountain is one of them. All those who have fallen and lived to describe their sensations are unanimous on one point — they experience no pain. And all who fell a considerable distance and expected to be killed experienced a feeling of detachment which was intermingled in some cases with sensations of petty annoyance and even of speculative interest. *(The Spirit of the Hills,* pp. 270f).

Not all of us can, like Smythe, look forward to death with interest and with a detachment which was possible to him because he had felt it, but we can seek to know as much as we can from the sources which are available. A number of other people have also had experiences which have taken them to the threshold of death and taught them that the actual experience of death, as distinct from the anticipation of it, is not in itself terrible. Of the nature of this experience we shall speak in the next chapter.

The Door of Death is made of gold
That mortal eyes cannot behold.
But when the mortal eyes are clos'd
And cold and pale the limbs repos'd,
The soul awakes, and, wond'ring sees
In her mild hand the golden Keys:
The Grave is heaven's Golden Gate,
And rich and poor around it wait;
O Shepherdess of England's fold,
Behold this Gate of Pearl and Gold!

William Blake

3 The Experience of Death

What does it feel like to die? For many people this may seem a very remote question, to others morbid, and to others again a presumption to think that one can give any answer to it at all. Yet it is neither irrelevant — for it will one day concern each of us — nor necessarily unhealthy — provided we do not allow ourselves to wallow in gloomy emotions — nor unanswerable — for there are, as I shall show, a number of sources of information. Before we can speak about this directly, however, it is necessary to consider what we think about the constitution of man. Any fundamental discussion of the basic facts of human existence leads inevitably to the question: What is Man? Is he just an advanced type of animal? Is he the product of purely mechanical, physical, chemical, biological processes? The outcome of the scientific inquiry as to the nature of humanity has been summed up by Bertrand Russell in the following words:

> That Man is the product of causes which had no prevision of the end they were achieving; that his origin, his growth, his hopes and fears, his loves and his beliefs, are but the outcome of accidental collocations of atoms; that no fire, no heroism, no intensity of thought and feeling can preserve an individual life beyond the grave; that all the labours of all the ages, all the devotion, all the inspiration, all the noonday brightness of human genius are destined to extinction in the vast death of the solar system, and that the whole temple of

> Man's achievement must inevitably be buried
> beneath the debris of a universe in ruins — all
> these things, if not quite beyond dispute, are yet so
> nearly certain that no philosophy which rejects
> them can hope to stand.

'All these things,' even if they are not absolutely certain, are the accepted view of millions of people in the world today, colouring their outlook and having consequences in their actions. But are they therefore necessarily true?

The diametrically opposite point of view is that of religion, which has hardly ever been more clearly or more concisely put than it was by the Psalmist when he said: 'Thou hast made him little less than God' (Thou makest him of almost godlike dignity)* and 'Thou hast put all things under his feet, all sheep and oxen, and also the beasts of the field, the birds of the air, and the fish of the sea.' (Psalm 8:5–7) He places humanity between the angels and the beasts, having something of the potentialities of both realms in them, yet not belonging wholly to either. It may not be entirely without significance that one frequently hears people say, without any serious thought behind their words: 'Be an angel!' or 'Don't be a beast!'

But let us hear now a man of this century who, speaking not out of any theoretical or theological ideas but directly out of an experience which led him to the limits of human endurance, is driven to ask: 'What am I?' This is Charles Lindbergh, the first man to fly the Atlantic alone, who described his sensations after eighteen hours' continuous flying:

* R. Frieling, *Hidden Treasures in the Psalms,* p.19.

After periods of crisis and many hours of fatigue, mind and body may become disunited until at times they seem completely different elements, as though the body were only a home with which the mind has been associated but by no means bound. Consciousness grows independent of the ordinary senses. You see without assistance from the eyes, over distances beyond the visual horizon. There are moments when existence appears independent even of the mind. The importance of physical desire and immediate surroundings is submerged in the apprehension of universal values.

For unmeasurable periods I seem divorced from my body, as though I were an awareness spreading out through space, over the earth and into the heavens, unhampered by time or substance, free from the gravitation that binds men to heavy human problems of the world. My body requires no attention. It is not hungry. It's neither warm nor cold. It's resigned to being left undisturbed. Why have I troubled to bring it here? I might better have left it back at Long Island or St Louis, while this weightless element that has lived within it flashes through the skies and views the planet. This essential consciousness needs no body for its travels. It needs no plane, no engine, no instruments, only the release from flesh which the circumstances which I have gone through make possible.

Then what am I — the body substance which I can see with my eyes and feel with my hands? Or am I this realization, this greater understanding which dwells within it, yet expands through the universe outside, a part of all existence ...?

It seems I'm made up of three personalities,

three elements, each partly dependent and partly independent of the others. There's my body, which knows definitely that what it wants most in the world is sleep. There's my mind, constantly making decisions that my body refuses to comply with, but which itself is weakening in resolution. And there's something else, which seems to become stronger instead of weaker with fatigue, an element of spirit, a directive force that has stepped out from the background and taken control over both mind and body. It seems to guard them as a wise father guards his children, letting them venture to the point of danger, then calling them back, guiding with a firm but tolerant hand. *(The Spirit of St Louis,* p.352.)

This description comes very close to the answer we would give from a modern Christian point of view; that the human being is a threefold being of body, soul, and an individual spirit. This last raises Man above the animals and renders him capable of being, at his best, 'of almost godlike dignity.' That which is truly 'I' in each of us stands in a certain relationship to him who said, 'I am the Light of the World.' Our soul expresses itself in the activities of thinking, feeling and will. The body can also be thought of as having three divisions: the head, containing the brain, the centre of the nervous system, as the physical organ of thinking and consciousness; the heart, and the circulation, together with the breathing — these together form the rhythmic element with which is associated our life of feeling; the digestive system, with all the lower organs, and the limbs, by which we outwardly express our will. The state of consciousness which we enjoy at any moment depends on the relationship between our spirit, soul and body and that relationship changes constantly. We have a different awareness of the world around us — and of people — according to our different states of health or sickness, or to varying atmospheric conditions, of hunger or comfort, or even according to the time of day. And the biggest change in that relationship is the one which takes place every night when we go to sleep and every morning when we wake up.

G.K. Chesterton once opened a radio talk by saying: 'Last night I died. This morning I was born again — to your great annoyance!' He was formulating in a rather dramatic way the often expressed thought that 'sleep is the little brother of death.' How far, on the basis of this thought, can we draw conclusions about the experience of death from what happens to us every night? At night that which is 'I" and that which is my soul go out of my body and leave it 'asleep.' If what is left behind were only the 'physical' body (using the word 'physical' as it is popularly used, as being synonymous with 'material') it would be not 'asleep' but dead, and there would be no waking up in the morning! It is 'asleep' because it is penetrated by a fourth member of the human constitution: the invisible body of etheric life forces. Its state is akin to that of the plants, not that of stones. The 'physical' body, together with its life-forces, is that which is left in the bed and to which we return in the morning.

What do we feel as this separation of our 'I' and our soul from our body takes place? Many people would say: 'I simply fall asleep,' or: 'I just drop off.' 'One moment I am here and the next moment I'm not.' It is difficult to catch what happens in that moment, but if we are attentive we may notice that our thoughts, as we think over the past day, become fuzzy at a certain point and we no longer control them. We pass over then to a series of pictures with no logical connection, we begin to dream. We do not as a rule remember these dream pictures in the morning because they are obliterated by the waking dream, but we can take over just sufficient consciousness to be aware of their beginning.

So in going to sleep our consciousness changes as our spirit and soul separate from our body with its life forces. We pass into dream consciousness, which we may or may not be able to recall afterwards, and then into sleep consciousness. Most people would call this unconsciousness, for who can tell apart from dreams, what experiences we have in sleep? But because we have no memory of them, must we assume that all consciousness is blotted out or that we cease to exist when we sleep?

Lindbergh could say of himself when he felt separated from his body: 'This essential consciousness needs no body for its travels.' Indeed this 'essential consciousness' travels free of the body when we are asleep, and the reason why we have no recollection of its experiences is that memory does require a connection with the body of life-forces, from which we are then separated. This 'life-body' is the storehouse of all the impressions and pictures from which our 'memories' are drawn, as it also is the source of our habitual actions which we perform without thinking. The waking dream reflects the moment of contact with this store of memory-pictures. If sleep represents a change in consciousness but not an extinction of it, is it not reasonable to think that death is similarly a change in consciousness but not an extinction of it?

This leads us back to the question: How can we know anything about what sort of consciousness exists beyond death? What does it feel like to die? In reply to this question, there are two main sources of knowledge: the evidence of those who having been brought through illness, accident or other circumstances to the threshold of death, have begun to cross it, but have then come back; and secondly, those rare persons whom we call initiates, those who while still on the Earth submit themselves, in one form or another, to a spiritual discipline and training which enables them to have direct and conscious experiences of the spiritual world (I leave aside for the moment the evidence of spiritualism, which will be considered later.)

Of those who have come back, many reports of their experiences have been recorded in the books of Dr Raymond Moody, to which reference will be made later. But for the moment let us consider the experiences of Charles Lindbergh, referred to above, which indicate the beginning of the separation of spirit and soul from the body in consequence of exhaustion and, particularly, through lack of sleep. For our ordinary well-being depends on our soul and spirit staying in the body only for a limited time before returning to the spiritual world for refreshment. If this refreshment is withheld, there is a tendency for our soul and spirit to withdraw by other means than the normal one of falling asleep. Lindbergh also makes it clear that there can be a consciousness which is detached from, instead of dependent on, the physical body. In normal states the physical body acts in a rather similar way to the white screen on to which slides or films are projected; without the screen there can be no clear pictures. The physical body is the basis of normal consciousness. What is the basis of body-free consciousness after death? With this question we shall deal in the next chapter.

Lindbergh speaks also of the phantoms of whose presence he became aware:

> [they] speak with human voices — friendly,
> vapour-like shapes, without substance, able to

vanish or appear at will, to pass in and out through the walls of the fuselage as though no walls were there. The spirits have no rigid bodies, yet they remain human in outline form — emanations from the experience of ages, inhabitants of a universe closed to mortal men. I'm on the borderline of life and a greater realm beyond, as though caught in the field of gravitation between two planets, acted on by forces I can't control, forces too weak to be measured by any means at my command, yet representing powers incomparably stronger than any I've yet known.

I realize that values are changing both within and without my mind. For twenty-five years, it's been surrounded by solid walls of bone, not perceiving the limitless expanse, the immortal existence that lies outside. Is this death? Am I crossing the bridge which one sees only in last, departing moments? Am I already beyond the point from which I can bring my vision back to earth and men? Death no longer seems the final end it used to be, but rather the entrance to a new and free existence which includes all space, all time.

Such experiences point to a possible extension of human awareness into spheres of existence which are independent of what happens to our body. They therefore support belief in a continuing, though changing, consciousness beyond death. They certainly create a different feeling towards death in all who have gone so close up to the threshold.

Frank Smythe contributes to this theme in his description of a fall which he had when climbing the Gröhmannspitze in the Dolomites with a friend. They were roped together and the friend stepped on a rock which gave way beneath him. His fall jerked Smythe from the ledge where he was standing and hurled him over the edge of the precipice. The rope, which had not been firmly secured, fortunately jammed in a crevice of rock and they both escaped with some scratches and bruises. Describing his sensations, Smythe wrote:

> In view of my subsequent sensations, the certainty which existed in my mind that nothing could stop me falling and that I was to be killed, is interesting and important. Nevertheless, even though I had assumed thus early that I was as good as dead, I made desperate attempts to stop myself ... During the time that I was doing this, a curious rigidity or tension gripped my whole mental and physical being. So great was this tension that it swamped all pain and fear, and rendered me insensible to bumps and blows. It was an overwhelming sensation, and quite outside my experience. It was as though all life's forces were in process of undergoing some fundamental evolutionary change, and the change called death, which is normally beyond imagination and outside the range of ordinary human force of power ... on the Gröhmannspitze I felt that power which alone can separate spirit from body — death. I know now that death is not to be feared, it is a supreme experience, the climax, not the anti-climax, of life.
>
> For how long I experienced this crescendo of power I cannot say. Time no longer existed as time; it was replaced by a sequence of events from which time as a quantity or quality in terms of human consciousness no longer existed. Then, suddenly,

this feeling was superseded by a feeling of complete indifference and detachment, indifference to what happened to my body, detachment from what was happening or likely to happen to that body. I seemed to stand aside from my body. I was not falling, for the reason that I was not in a dimension where it was possible to fall. I, that is my consciousness, was apart from my body, and not in the least concerned with what was befalling it. My body was in the process of being injured, crushed and pulped, and my consciousness was not associated with these physical injuries, and was completely uninterested in them. Had the tenant already departed in anticipation of the wreck that was to follow? Had the assumption of death — when my slide was not checked by the rope I assumed death as certain — resulted in a partial dissolution of the spiritual and physical? Was it merely a mental effect due to a sudden and intense nervous strain? It is not within my province to discuss that which only death can prove; yet to me this experience was a convincing one; it convinced me that consciousness survives beyond the grave. (*The Spirit of the Hills,* pp. 279–81.)

But let us consider what is the actual process of change by which the soul and spirit take leave of the body — a process which is in principle the same whether it happens quickly, as in accidental or sudden death, or slowly, as in old age or illness.

The ancient peoples had, in some respects, a much clearer idea of the process than we have today, though this arose from a quite different general state of human consciousness. The Egyptians spoke of the *ka* of a person, which left the body at death. This *ka* was not just the soul of the deceased, which hovered in birdlike form above the mummified body, but had connection also with the life-forces. Therefore a person could experience bodily existence only so long as he had connection with his *ka.*

For the Greeks the *psyche* was connected with the breathing and rhythmic system and was breathed out through the mouth and nostrils when a person died. It was regarded as the invisible image, or *eidolon,* of the body, which became visible only at death, and this was depicted in Greek art as a little figure coming out of the mouth of the dead. This rightly portrays the withdrawal of the soul through the head, in particular through the sense-organs: eyes, ears, and so on.

Of those who have deliberately crossed the threshold and come back again, able to describe what they felt, a striking experience of Paul Brunton* is worth noting. After having studied and gained some proficiency in yoga practice in India, he went to Egypt and decided he would try and investigate the spiritual phenomena of the pyramids by these methods. It was an undertaking fraught with no little risk, for not a few have lost their lives in mysterious ways in connection with the pyramids. It was not without difficulty, therefore, that he got permission from the Curator of Antiquities in Cairo to spend a night alone in one of the pyramids. In the absolute silence and darkness of the tomb he soon became aware of the presence of invisible beings whom he sensed as being hostile and seeking to frighten him away. But he resisted this suggestion and, laying himself on a raised stone slab, he proceeded, by the yoga methods he was trained in, to withdraw himself (that is to say his 'I,' his soul and his life

* *A Search in Secret Egypt.*

forces) from his body. He suspended the functioning of his bodily processes. He proceeded to 'die.' As he could maintain a full consciousness of what was happening to him, he could record afterwards his exact sensations. First, a coldness spread from his legs upwards into his body, gradually paralysing it as life withdrew from it. When this process reached the heart it caused a spasm, similar to a severe heart attack. This, however, he could master and the process continued up to the head. Here for a time there was a sensation of terrific pressure, until suddenly something took place like the air rushing out of a pricked balloon — and he felt a great expansion and a great relief as the release from the body took place. He was now free in the soul world and could look down on his body, lying as if dead on the slab in the tomb. Connecting him with it was a thread of light — his life-line. So long as that was unbroken he could get back into his body again; if anything happened to break it, then there would be no possibility of return, and he would be truly dead.

He then goes on to describe his meeting with the spirit of an ancient Egyptian priest, but with this we are not concerned here. What is of interest is the conscious experience of the process of dying, though one should not think that the same sensations will be felt by everyone in dying. Apart from the different causes of death (illness, accident, and so on), everyone has a different constitution; that is to say, the degree of connection between the four constituent members: spirit (or 'I'), soul, life-body and physical body can vary greatly. Some people sit firmly and solidly in their body (the more phlegmatic type), others are more loosely connected (often 'cholerics') and are by nature more inclined to 'pass out.' The persistent practice of meditation can make it easier for the soul to free itself from the body, while some illnesses bind it more tightly.

Turning to more recent literature on the subject, many of these experiences are confirmed in the hundreds of accounts collected by Dr Raymond Moody and published in his widely-read book, *Life after Life*. Two images seem to dominate what is related. One is 'the dark tunnel,' the other is 'the figure of Light.' The dark tunnel appears to mark the beginning of the withdrawal of the soul and the loosening of the etheric body from the physical. Even this is not final and can be reversed. The descriptions of this tunnel-experience vary. For some it is a quiet peaceful experience with no feeling of fear; for some a dark void in which they tumble about; for some a long dark tube into which they just fit and travel through at great speed, in some cases accompanied by a rhythmic humming noise; others liken it to a very deep dark valley and think of it as the valley of the shadow of death. But at the end of the tunnel is always the light of the spiritual world. (A somewhat similar experience is described by Laurens van der Post at the end of his novel, *In a Province.)*

Two things stand out from nearly all these experiences. Firstly that the release of the soul from the body brings a feeling of happiness and well-being. Particularly must this be so after illnesses which have involved much suffering, but it is something far transcending the mere relief from pain. Secondly, that the world immediately beyond the threshold is one of light. As the soul begins withdrawing from the body, a dying person can sometimes look across into that world of light and even describe what is seen. Sometimes angel forms are visible or those of loved ones waiting to greet them. These can be very precious experiences for the relatives and friends as they stand at the bedside. Their darkness too is relieved by those gleams.

One other experience is brought back by many who have nearly died: that of the life-panorama. This is released by the shock of knowing that death is imminent. People who have been half-drowned and then rescued just in time have described how, in the moment when their lungs filled with water and they gave up all hope of survival, scenes from their life unfolded themselves before their soul with an astonishing vividness. All was bathed in a bright light and a sense of great peace and bliss filled them. In some cases the pictures unrolled in order backwards to the person's childhood — in other cases more haphazardly. These are only very fragmentary glimpses of a wider and more impressive life-panorama which the soul has after death and which will be described more fully in the next chapter.

We find also in Dr George Ritchie's account of his personal experience of 'near death' *(Return from Tomorrow)* the question which he feels put to him by this 'figure of light' concerning his life: 'What did you do with your life?' or 'How much have you loved with your life?' In this a kind of self-judgment arose which was combined with the beginning of the life-panorama. 'Every detail of twenty years of living was there to be looked at, the good, the bad, the high points, the run-of-the-mill.' In addition the figure of light (whom Ritchie identifies as 'Lord Jesus') shows Ritchie the fate of those who, having died, are still obsessed with their craving for drink, cigarettes or other earthly pleasures but have no longer the means to satisfy it. He realizes that this is what 'hell' really is.

Besides the reports of those who have 'been dead' and come back, in regard to which the books of Dr Moody and Dr Ritchie are popular and widely read modern examples, there is another source of information which comes to us 'from the other side.' I am not referring to the mediumistic communications of spiritualists. That is a separate subject. But there are certain individuals whom we call 'sensitives' whose soul perceptions are, through some fact in their destiny, open to receive in full consciousness messages from certain individuals in the spiritual world with whom they are closely connected. Mostly they are intimate communications which do not reach the printed page.

Occasionally however there is an impulse, or even a command, to publish such information about what lies beyond death, for the good of humanity. Naturally one examines carefully and critically the credentials and motives of those who publish such information. There have been two such books published within the last fifteen years which have come my way and of whose genuineness I am convinced.

The first, *The Bridge over the River,* concerns communications from the life after death of a young artist called Sigwart, who died in the First World War at the age of thirty-one. The young man was a promising musician and had three sisters, with one of whom he was specially connected and with whom he managed after a time to establish communication. She described it to one of her sisters: 'I have come to recognize what Sigwart expects of me, which is not to guide my hand and influence it externally; rather, I myself must open a door in my mind; then I shall hear the words I have to write down.' Later on in 1932 a message was received from Sigwart's 'Masters' saying: 'What he has been permitted to convey to you should now be disseminated in order to bestow blessings, to heal sorrow and to point the way to the light. *The Time is at hand.*'

It is clear from the book that it is by no means to be taken for granted that the dead are permitted to make such communications even when it is possible. There must be present not just human desire but a willingness to be used as a channel for the spiritual world.

The second book to which I would refer, and which has given me much joy, is *The Testimony of Light* by Helen Greaves. Here we have someone who had been intensively engaged in religious work together with her friend, Frances Banks, who was for twenty-five years a sister in the Community of the Resurrection in South Africa and for much of that time Principal of the Teachers' Training College in Grahamstown. They explored together deep levels of meditation and so were closely joined in life through their spiritual seeking. Frances Banks died and, three weeks later, Helen Greaves felt the presence of her friend as she sat by the fire listening to radio music, and entered into a state of communion with her.

> It was some days later when I felt Frances' *mind* impinging in mine as it had often done in our time together on earth. Words dropped into my thoughts which did not come from my consciousness. I knew that her discarnate mind and my incarnate one had linked together again in telepathic communication ... I sat down, took my pen and began to write. Words, thoughts and sentences tumbled out onto the paper. It was almost as though I took dictation. Yet this was *not* automatic writing. I was perfectly in control. I could *feel* that her mind was using mine. This was a composite effort. Her mind 'inspired' the subject matter, the experiences and, later, the stories of her fellow-travellers in the Life Beyond. She explored the potentials of my mind and enabled me to employ the craft of writing which I had learned in my journalistic work.

Frances Banks lays emphasis on the importance of the groups to which we belong naturally or by destiny in our earthly life and to which soul groups we are drawn in the life beyond.

> First of all we belong to a Family Group, we are born into and marry into Family Groups which are most suitable for the type of experience and lessons we, as incarnating souls, need ... This first is the simplest Group and many souls remain under the joyful protection and guidance of this Group Being for a long span. The next Groups are the Groups of interest, passionate attachments to the arts, music, education, social sciences and social service ... Such Groups would be those of musicians, artists, prophets, orators, writers, doctors, philosophers, scientists who had passed through the Group Work and graduated. Their passionate interest would naturally be part of their soul life and they would graduate to such Groups where they could continue their studies and their achievements.

There are also higher Groups of extended consciousness to which souls gradually advance as they become fit to do so.

> All is progress. Nothing is static. Imagination passes and grows from the emotional to the mental to the spiritual levels. Life is a continuing Path towards one's particular Group, one's individual experiences, one's own progress and onwards into the arc of ascendancy. [To me this is a far more heartening process than any glory of a static heaven with angels

and golden floors.] Angels of course there are: great
Beings of Light who do the Will of the Divine
Creator and who carry and transmit: Power and
Beauty and Light.

Frances Banks speaks of sloughing off (like a snake its
skin) those parts of personality which are related to Earth
existence and which have clothed and concealed the true
self, the reality of being and that true self she describes as
'substantial light.' It is understandable therefore that the
book is called *The Testimony of Light.*

Such, in brief, are some of the facts about the experience of death which those who are still alive in the body
can bring back from their brush with death.

But let us now consider what can be learned from a
teacher who has been termed, in the title of A.P.
Shepherd's book about him, *A Scientist of the Invisible.**
Rudolf Steiner was not, like Paul Brunton , an exponent
of a westernized form of yoga, nor did he derive his
knowledge from any sort of mediumistic communications, but rather through an extension of the normal
process of knowledge and investigation along scientific
lines to include phenomena perceivable in full consciousness only by means of systematically developed spiritual
faculties. This knowledge he called spiritual science, or
anthroposophy. The means by which anyone who has sufficient determination, moral strength of character and
interest in spiritual things, can develop such powers, is
described in many of his writings. It must, however, be
said that the path by which these powers are achieved is
longer and harder than anyone thinks at the outset, and it

---

* To many readers the name of Rudolf Steiner will be familiar and need
no introduction. To others A.P. Shepherd's book, as also *Rudolf Steiner
Enters my Life* by Friedrich Rittelmeyer, may be recommended.

is only a small number of those who attempt to do so who achieve them in any high degree.

By these means Rudolf Steiner was able to investigate or look into (quite literally) spheres of existence not accessible to our ordinary senses, and, in regard to our subject, it means that he could describe facts about death and what lies beyond which could not otherwise be known. This is a claim which may well appear incredible and preposterous to some, but let it be considered that his statements need be accepted with just as little — or as much — credulity as is given to pronouncements by advanced physicists or other experts in their own fields. The 'man in the street' cannot verify them; he can accept, or reject, them in his own mind. Only an expert of equal standing can verify the pronouncement. Such is the situation with Steiner's statements. But he always emphasized that they should be considered, without prejudice, as hypotheses, not as dogmas: ordinary human common sense can judge whether or not such spiritual hypotheses make sense in relation to the experienced facts of existence.

A great deal of what is contained in the following chapter is derived from this source of knowledge and such information is important, not because it represents an interesting or curious new 'theory,' nor because it is of an extraordinary nature, but because it is vitally necessary that in an age in which attitudes towards death have become increasingly materialistic, more and more people should know about the spiritual facts of death and life after death — facts which have always been known to seers and initiates.

*That is what modern initiation science must bring —
understanding of the Christ. We need an initiation science that can penetrate again into the spiritual world,
that can speak again about birth and death about the
life between birth and death and the life also between
death and a new birth, and about the life of the soul in
sleep. The possibility must be there for man to come
again to a knowledge of the other side — the spiritual
side of existence. Otherwise he will simply not be able
to go forward into the future.*

Rudolf Steiner, *Man's Life on Earth*

*Because man goes to his eternal home, and the mourn-
ers go about the streets; before the silver cord is
snapped, or the golden bowl is broken, or the pitcher is
broken at the fountain, or the wheel broken at the cis-
tern, and the dust returns to the earth as it was, and the
spirit returns to God who gave it.*

Ecclesiastes 12:5–7

4 After Death

What are the experiences of the soul when once 'the silver cord is loosed,' when the body is finally laid aside and the threshold of death is crossed?* Firstly, there is the feeling of release, of joyous freedom from the restrictions of the body, of a great expansion into a world of light. This, strange to say, results from that turning inwards of consciousness of the dying person which seems to those standing at the death-bed as a fading away of consciousness. In fact, it is an exchanging of an awareness of the physical world around for an inner awareness, the sort of awareness which we cultivate in intensive prayer and meditation — a form of 'active inwardness.' Then before this 'inner awareness' there rise up pictures of our past life, not just memories, such as we have in ordinary life, and not just one after the other in a time sequence, but as a series of living pictures of all the events of our past life, one beside the other and around us on all sides, so that we feel ourselves in the centre of our memories. Yet they are not just memories but immediate experiences.

'There I am as a child of seven, playing happily in the garden ... there, when I am in my teens, are my parents, sad and worrying because I am being deceitful over something I do not wish them to know about ... there I am as a young man, flushed with pride and a bit 'cocky' over the first success of my career ... there I am in despair over the difficulties of a human situation out of which I

* The following brief account is based on the extensive spiritual researches of Rudolf Steiner. For fuller details, see the Bibliography.

cannot see my way ...' and so on. In the midst of all these *tableaux vivants* we live for the first three to four days after death.

These images of our past life have been impressed into our 'life-body.' This is nothing physical, but an invisible, intangible structure of forces which are conveniently described with the word 'etheric.' The form of this 'body' is not static, yet, though flexible, it has a certain permanence. To understand this one might think of those great white cumulus clouds one sees on a summer day, whose forms appear so sharply defined against the blue sky. Yet their substance is in constant movement.

In this invisible, intangible body are stored up all our memories, all our experiences in life, whether great or small. When we 'remember' some past event, we drink at the pool of memory. This is the sphere of the sub-conscious, from which the psychologists tell us that nothing is ever lost, and from which the long-forgotten can be raised up. This is the sphere in which our dream-images are stored up, which flash up incoherently, without the direction of the conscious mind, when we dream.

During life this etheric body is compressed by the physical body into something like the same space as itself, but at death, released from this pressure, it expands rapidly and vastly. To use a very trivial illustration: think of a silk handkerchief squeezed into a very tight ball within one's hand; release it, and it very quickly billows out to something like its full size. The soul now lives for normally three to four days surrounded by this great panorama of memory pictures. Yet they are not just like grey shadows as memories mostly are. They are intensely vivid experiences, full of colour, full of feeling and emotion. Rudolf Steiner describes:

We live for days 'inside' our experiences.
Simultaneously in mighty pictures there is the event
which we have just experienced in the last days
before death and simultaneously there is present
what we have experienced in childhood ... All that
we see lives in the ether. Above all we feel what is
around us is alive. And we experience it as spiritually sounding, spiritually shining, and also spiritually warming. This life-tableau disappears after
some days. But what is this life-tableau? If one
investigates this life-tableau as to what it really is,
one must say: into it is woven all that we have I
experienced in life. But experienced how? In that
we have thought with it. All that we experienced in
thinking, imagining, that is contained in it. ('The
Ego-consciousness of the so-called Dead.')

This, however, is only the first stage, and reaches its
end as the life-forces dissolve from the body and are
absorbed into the universe. Then comes the great expansion of the soul into the soul world. This brings with it
such an overwhelming extension of consciousness that it
is as if one were led out of a completely dark, small cham-
ber into a vast hall, blazing with thousands of dazzling
lights. We are dazed. We have to struggle to adjust to this
condition of excessive consciousness. We have to find our
bearings. This corresponds to what the Greeks knew as
the plunge into the stream of Lethe, the river of forget-
fulness, and the awakening on the further shore.

When we reach that stage of 'awakening on the further
shore,' we have to learn to adjust ourselves to a radically
different outlook on existence. While we are on Earth, we
look out into the universe from one particular point,
which is the one where our body happens to be, because

it is only through having a body that we are conscious of ourselves. So we say: I am here, in my body, and around me is the world and the sky, the planets and stars and all space. After death — that is, after our physical body is given back to the elements of the earth, whether in the grave or by cremation, and the life-forces have dissolved into the universe — then our soul also expands and spreads itself out, as it were, over a (spiritually) vast part of the universe. It is no longer tied to one spot by the body. But, being thus diffused, our problem is to find ourselves; and what we seek is a focusing point.

It is in some ways a comparable problem, at least as far as our human thinking is concerned, to that which we have in trying to grasp with our minds the 'omnipresence' of Christ. How, we may ask, can Christ be accessible to all men everywhere at the same time? It is difficult, of course, out of our natural instinct to think of him still in terms of bodily existence. But if, on the other hand, we say to ourselves: No, he is spirit, then we may merely be escaping into an abstraction. If we can understand the Ascension as the moment when Christ made himself part of 'the heavenly forces on earth' — and not only part of, but Lord of those forces, which by their heavenly nature transcend the laws of natural science — then, by that transcendent quality he can focus and manifest his presence at every Christian altar where his name is invoked and where true sacraments are performed. Difficult as this thought may be, it is a sort of foretaste of the kind of adjustment we have to make after death, and it is in this adjusting that the power of the resurrected and ascended Christ comes to our aid, when we then have to acquire 'omnipresence' and find means of 'focusing' in order to become aware of ourselves (We may remember, too, that a baby's eyes do not at first focus; they look out beyond space. No real earthly consciousness begins until the eyes focus and the child begins to see the world.)

The greatest of the experiences on which we look back is the moment of death itself. It is 'the point which leaves behind it the very deepest impression for the whole of life between death and new birth; it is the point that is remembered most of all ... The moment of death is something that is looked back upon with a deep sense of blessing.' (Rudolf Steiner)

This is the 'golden gate' aspect of death; the gate which looks so dark and forbidding from this side proves, when we have gone through it, to be of solid gold. It is the different point of view that makes all the difference. 'The soul awakes and wondering sees. In her mild hand the golden keys.' These are the keys to body-free self-consciousness. I know I am 'I' in the soul world because I look back at the Golden Gate of Death and know that I have 'died.' Strange as it may seem, the soul of a person who has died suddenly, for instance in a crash, may not realize the fact of death but, seeing the wreck, tries to help in rescuing other victims of the disaster, and cannot understand that no one sees them or takes any notice. Dr Moody gives an example: 'People were walking up from all directions to get to the wreck. I could see them and I was in the middle of a very narrow walkway. Anyway as they came by they wouldn't seem to notice me. They would just keep walking with their eyes straight ahead. As they came real close I would try to turn around to get out of their way but they would just walk *through* me.'

Perhaps because of the possibility of such unawareness, Christians have prayed: 'From sudden death, good Lord, deliver us.' The conscious experience of the moment of death is valuable from this point of view, though modern thought and practice run counter to such a view. While the use of morphia and other pain-killing drugs is to a certain point desirable and merciful to relieve unbearable pain, their indiscriminate use robs people of at least part of the 'golden gate' experience after death.

As we have said, we cannot at first perceive the spiritual world clearly because our faculties are not trained for perceiving in these quite different conditions. The faculty of seeing in the soul-world is dependent on certain things in our life on Earth. These can be summed up in the words: Love of the Spirit. There is a lower part of our soul which is attracted to the delights of the physical world, the pleasures of our bodily senses, but there is also a higher part of our soul which takes pleasure in the things of the spirit. Much depends after death on which of these two has governed our life. In this connection it is significant that in more than one prayer given by Rudolf Steiner for children we find the words: 'I love the Spirit of God.' The same thought occurs in the Burial Service of The Christian Community. It is our love of spiritual things, of beauty, truth and goodness, that develops in us the organ of spiritual perception after death.

But to get our eyes working, as it were, we need something to focus on, so our awakening power of perception seeks something that it knows. But this can only be something which represents a reality in the world we have now reached — an experience of spiritual significance. We may think here of moments when we have felt the presence of Christ at the altar, or of occasions in prayer or meditation when for a short while we have reached the heights. These now light up for us like spiritual beacon lights from which we may get our bearings. We identify the spiritual lighthouses which we have ourselves built during our earthly life, and by them, like the captain of a ship, we know where we are. Two further helps we have:

the earnest prayers of our friends still on Earth; their intercession comes to us like a familiar fragrance. And then the welcoming by our friends and loved ones already 'on the other side.' Our approach to and passing through the gate of death will have been watched by them with loving interest. Rudolf Steiner wrote: '... the question: shall I see again after death those with whom I have felt myself connected in the world of sense experience? — must be answered from the side of a real research, which is entitled in this sphere to a judgement out of experience, with a decisive, "Yes".' So we find ourselves in adjusting to a new kind of consciousness.

But having lived over into this new consciousness, what do we then do? What tasks has the soul then to embark on once it has reached the far shore?

In the theology of the Middle Ages, and of the Roman Catholic Church today, much was made of the doctrine of purgatory, the place of cleansing fire which every soul must pass through on its way to heaven. A lot was said about the sufferings to be endured in this place, as also in hell, thus introducing the element of fear into the sphere of religious discipline, a factor which was exploited by not too scrupulous priests. Vivid pictures arising from the doctrine will come to the mind of anyone who has read even a little of Dante's *Divine Comedy*.

The Reformers rejected this doctrine on the grounds that it was unscriptural (though the parable of the Rich Man and Lazarus would seem to point to some kind of purgatorial state), and put their emphasis on 'justification by faith.' The picture in this case was rather that of the law court, where man had to justify himself before God.

Yet if one thinks basically and simply of the nature of man as a being of spiritual origin and having a spiritual kernel to his being, who inhabits for a limited span of time a physical body and whose soul is coloured during that time by all the experiences, sensations and desires which arise from having such a body built of the substance of earth and thereby involving him in earthly processes — should not such a soul need some cleansing process before being returned to a realm of pure spirit?

Our imagination may be helped here by the picture of the soul-garments which are referred to in various places in the New Testament. The parable of the King's Wedding Feast (Matthew 22) comes to mind, in which the crucial question is: 'How did you get in here without a wedding garment?' We may not enter the highest spiritual presence unless our soul is properly clothed. So Paul, too, writes to the Corinthians: 'Here indeed we groan, and long to put on our heavenly dwelling, so that by putting it on we may not be found naked. For while we are still in this tent, we sigh with anxiety; not that we would be unclothed, but that we would be further clothed, so that what is mortal may be swallowed up by life.' (2Cor.5:2–4). This again points to the transformation which the soul needs in order to stand worthily before God. Or the great pictures of the Book of Revelation rise up before us: ' "Who are these, clothed in white robes, and whence have they come?" I said to him, "Sir, you know." And he said to me, "These are they who have come out of the great tribulation; they have washed their robes and made them white in the blood of the Lamb".' (7:13f)

In the course of living on the Earth we experience much that is 'tribulation': we rub up against much that is, from a high spiritual point of view, impure, and through that our soul-garments get discoloured. Instead of showing to the angelic world pure shining colours of gold or blue or delicate pink, our garments are streaked with muddy browns and reds, dirty greens and yellows. Think only of two people having a blazing row and calling each other vile names, surely their soul-garments are mud-bespattered and much in need of cleaning afterwards! But that is only a crude example. In ways so fine and subtle that we are not aware of them our souls get impregnated with earthly thoughts, earthly desires and earthly impulses.

When we die, we go into the other world with all that we have become through these experiences and, for the eyes of the spiritual beings, we must appear rather 'out-landishly dressed' when we arrive. Many of our garments will have to be laid aside because they are out of place. The stripping off of these garments takes place in seven stages. A picture for this is that the soul divests herself of seven veils until she stands naked before God. In the description given by spiritual science these stages are described as seven regions, or elements, through which the soul passes and in each of which it stays a shorter or longer time according to its relationship to that region. If it corresponds to a form of inclination, or desire to which the soul was much attached in earthly life, then the soul stays there until that attachment is dissolved. If it was an element in life in which the soul had little interest, then it passes quickly through.

In the first stages the soul is concerned with eliminating those desires which can only be satisfied through having a physical body. We inevitably suffer if we have desires but no possibility of fulfilling them. The desires burn us. Therefore the more we free ourselves of such desires before we die, the less we shall have to suffer in this region. At the other end of the scale are feelings and impulses towards the Earth so refined that we reckon them here on Earth as virtues; for example, our love of the beauty of Earth. Even this must be laid aside in order that we may devote ourselves wholly to the spirit. (Rudolf Steiner warns us that these 'regions ' must not be thought of as spatially separate, not as successive to one another in time, but rather as co-terminous and simultaneous. But it is to be remembered that the soul is now independent of space and time.)

In this soul-world something else is also taking place, and I that is that we live backwards through the events of our past life, seeing and feeling them not as we saw and felt them at the time, but rather in a mirror, as reflected through the eyes of those who were affected by our deeds and words. Of all the actions we do in the world we are only aware of what the action means for us — that it gives us satisfaction, or that we feel we did it badly, or that it was very boring to do it. In so far as it affects other people we have little possibility of knowing what it has meant for them. If we are sensitive, we may have an inkling of how they have taken it, but not a complete realization of their experience. It may have been quite different from what we have imagined it to be. In the soul-world after death we shall know. We shall feel now what they felt then. Every hasty, unkind, careless word comes back to us now and we experience in ourselves the effect it had on the other. It needs little imagination to realize what feelings of regret and remorse must arise from this experience. The purgatorial character of this is clear and the prospect of it enjoins on us a far greater responsibility for all that we do and say in this life than we normally feel. The other side of the picture, however, is that we experience the joys, pleasures and comforts we have given other people, sometimes without fully realizing how much they mean to them, and maybe we shall be surprised at some of the people who will appear to rise up and bless us.

In the course of these experiences we feel arising in us impulses to repair what was done wrong, to do better what was inadequate, and to do good to those whom our actions and words had injured. Yet we can do nothing about it. For we are not in a condition of freedom; that we have only on the Earth. Here we are dealing solely with effects brought about by the operation of spiritual law, springing from causes which we have set in motion on the Earth. We cannot change the effects, we can only suffer them. Yet the impulses we receive to put things right are not lost: they are stored up for us and form part of a future destiny. For that is the wonderful thing about life on this Earth, that we have the power of freedom to change the world around us, to change human relationships. However circumscribed our position in life may seem, we can have an effect on it, if not outwardly and visibly, at least spiritually because of what we are. Therefore, having seen the effects of our past life, we already experience the wish to come once again to Earth. But first we must go further and undergo a most fundamental process of change.

Any attempt to describe the world of life after death must inevitably be fragmentary and one-sided. Rudolf Steiner described it on different occasions from many different aspects and always stressed the inadequacy of human concepts and words to convey the spiritual realities. So we need to supplement the sketch of the inner experiences of the human spirit after death with some view of the cosmic spheres in which they take place.

Early Christian and medieval religious thought spoke of the 'seven heavens' — St Paul mentions being 'caught up to the third heaven' (2Cor.12:2) — and some painters have even attempted to depict this. One miniature, entitled 'The Earthly Paradise,' from a series called 'The Seven Ages of the World,' painted by Simon Marion about 1460, depicts Adam and Eve in a parklike landscape with a deer, a lion, a swan and other creatures, quite naturalistically drawn, but above them are indicated the seven planetary spheres from the Moon upwards to the realm of the fixed stars. Beyond that, God the Father on his throne dominates the entire picture, surrounded by a sphere of red and gold, shot through with rays of heavenly light and encircled by triple ranks of angelic beings. In this painting the natural world is shown as an appendage of the heavenly world, and to ponder this is no bad exercise to correct our over-materialistic way of thinking today. It also gives, at least symbolically, a picture of the cosmic spheres through which the human soul and spirit go after death.

Again it must be said that all our earthly concepts arise out of our living in space and living in time. Since after death we are no longer in space and time, the conditions of existence are strictly speaking not describable in earthly terms at all. It might be thought then that in speaking of such things we are talking in mere abstractions. Rudolf Steiner, however, emphasizes that the spiritual facts and experiences are real, though in a different dimension. They can only be described in terms of: 'it is as if ...' The soul has an experience 'as if it were speaking with a friend,' 'as if it were being looked at by many people,' and so on. Particularly words of place, as sphere, realm, planet, and so on, must be understood as comparisons only. The soul after death does not visit the planets like the modern astronaut or cosmonaut. What is visible through the telescope is no more than a marker or signpost in space which indicates an invisible and spiritual sphere of existence. When Christ said: 'In my Father's house are many mansions,' he was also describing spiritual realities in earthly terms.

The interests which we have while here in our earthly body do not cease with death. We continue to have the same habits of thought and feeling and if they have been self-centred in life, they will continue to be so and will repel much that approaches the soul in its new state. We want to do the same things but the body as an instrument of the soul is no longer available. The soul therefore experiences insatiable desires. In earthly terms we would call this frustration, and from this frustration the soul suffers. It has to spend a time in learning to go without what can be only satisfied through the body.

The other side of the picture is that our souls also have spiritual desires. It is these that will connect us with the next higher world and will lead us to make progress in the soul world. Every longing for truth, beauty and goodness, and, above all, our love for Christ will lead us onward.

The daily life of our soul when we are on Earth is made up of innumerable sense impressions which our eyes record, our ears hear, our tongue tastes, and so on. It is the variety of these impressions, trivial and unimportant though they may be in themselves, which make us feel that we are alive. Any one impression may please or displease us, may arouse feelings of sympathy or antipathy in us, but at least we know that we are alive. We now experience the spiritual counterpart of the streaming, flowing forces of earthly life but now not as something outside us but as a kind of circulation of spiritual forces within the soul.

In earthly life, apart from responding to stimulation from without, we also have impulses out of ourselves to do something, to be active, to be creative. We may wish to learn a foreign language, to study music, to do social

work, or to work in the garden — these and many other
wishes and impulses make up a large part of our soul life.
Our inner activity of wishing finds expression in outer
activities for which we use our physical body. In the spiritual world this wish activity continues to stream out in all
directions from the soul seeking satisfaction. The selfish
element in this has also to be overcome if we are to make
progress.

All these processes take place while the soul is in the
spiritual sphere of the Moon, the planet which was once
part of the Earth and which, in the processes of birth and
death is a kind of antechamber to the Earth for the soul
seeking incarnation and an antechamber to the spiritual
world for the departing soul.

Beyond this the soul enters the cosmic sphere of
Mercury and enters into a new relationship with the
Angels, Archangels and the Archai, who are the Spirits of
Time. He receives instruction from them in the understanding of the realities of the spiritual world, but in this
he will be greatly hindered if his thinking on the Earth has
been of an entirely materialistic kind, having no place for
any realities which cannot be perceived with our ordinary
five senses. Nor will he be able to perceive his spiritual
instructors, or other souls around him, if he has not
developed his moral qualities to a sufficient degree.
Immorality during life causes the individual to experience
'solitary confinement' in this sphere.

In the Venus sphere, where the forces of cosmic love
meet us, these will be transformed, for the soul not yet
purged of all hatred, into wrath. He will experience the
'wrath of God,' not in the sense of personal anger on the
part of the deity (he is not an angry God, but a God of
love), but as a turbulent storm arising within himself.
Cosmic love is a force which we cannot stand if we are

not attuned to it. If we are in the wrong key, it sounds to us like a clashing discord. But in the Venus sphere we shall find ourselves in communion with those people with whom in our earth life we could share our religious thoughts and experiences. Here we shall know the true meaning of religious community and feel it as the greatest joy.

With the Sun sphere we reach the last of the seven stages of the purification of the soul. Here the last traces of attachment to the Earth vanish. We now reach the heart of the universe where the Christ unites all humankind. 'We feel ourselves one with the whole wide universe; and what we were before on Earth — that we feel as something outside us. The whole universe is reflected in us as in an eye of the spirit, and we feel ourselves one with the destinies which we have experienced both in ourselves and in other human souls.'

Through all these spheres we are being worked on and transformed by spiritual beings from the ranks of the nine hierarchies — from the Angels up to the Seraphim. They are preparing the spiritual seed of what we shall be in our next incarnation. So our evolution is a continuous one under the direction of these higher powers. From birth to death and from death to a new birth the process goes on. In the Sun sphere we come under the influence of the second hierarchy, that is, with the middle three ranks of the nine: the Mights, Powers and Dominions, as they are known in Christian terminology (in the Christmas liturgy of The Christian Community they are named the Revealers, the World-Powers, the World-Guides).*

Beyond the Sun sphere we advance into the spirit-land proper — as distinct from the soul-world — and come

* Their Greek names are: *Exousiai, Dynameis, Kyriotetes.*

into the planetary spheres of Mars, Jupiter and Saturn. Here we are really led 'behind the scenes' of the universe and are shown the archetypes of all that exists on the Earth.

What do we mean by 'archetype'? Before a picture is painted, the idea of the picture exists in the artist's mind. He does not see it down to the last detail; much of that will come to him as he paints, but the idea is there. An architect designs a house. Long before it gets on the drawing board he has a picture in his mind of how it will look and its main features. If he builds several houses they may all be based on the same 'idea' but work out with slight variations as they are built. So for everything natural on the Earth, all living things, plants, rocks, minerals, there is an idea, an archetype in the spiritual world which may project itself on to the Earth in a variety of different forms. There exists an archetype of a butterfly — but how varied in their beauty are all the different sorts of butterfly!

We meet the archetypes of the minerals, the stones and the crystals (in the Mars region), the archetypes of all varieties of plants (in the Jupiter region) and the archetypes of the different species of animals (in the Saturn region).

That spiritual patterns, or archetypes, exist for all things on the Earth is hinted at in Exodus 25, where God directs Moses to fashion the tabernacle and its fittings 'after the pattern for them, which is being shown you on the mountain.' On Sinai, Moses was given a vision into the world of the archetypes.

Christ himself created an archetype of true prayer when the disciples asked him: 'Lord, teach us to pray,' and he gave them what we know as the Lord's Prayer. This was also a 'pattern which was shown on the moun-

tain' and to which we can always turn if we want to know
how to pray truly.

So, too, there is an archetype of divine worship which
exists as a blueprint in the spiritual world. From it various
projections have been made throughout man's history,
and from it a fresh image was projected on to this Earth
for this age when the new form of the Communion
Service, the Act of Consecration of Man, was revealed
and given through the agency of Rudolf Steiner, acting as
a servant of the divine powers.

In the Mars sphere also are to be found the origins of
the faculty of speech — the gift which the divine beings
have bestowed only on the human being amongst all the
creatures of the Earth. That Adam was able to give names
to all the creatures indicate how the faculty of speech is
connected with creation. Speech in its spiritual sense is
creative. In our modern abuse and misuse of words this
has been forgotten; perhaps only the poets still feel it. Yet
St John could write: 'In the beginning was the Word ...
and the Word was God.'

In the Jupiter sphere we encounter thoughts as living
realities, not as pale, abstract images, as human thoughts
mostly are, but as thoughts of the gods. The world of
spirit is woven out of the substance of which human
thought consists. Here we perceive the truths, the secret
wisdom on which the universe is founded.

Saturn, the last of the planetary spheres, is the great
archivist of the universe. Here is the region of world-mem-
ory, where everything that ever happened still is. If we
imagine the recording angels writing the deeds of men into
their records, this is the 'place' where those records are
kept — a far vaster store than the contents of all the muse-
ums, libraries and archives that the world has ever seen.
The fundamental fact of memory springs from this source.

In these last three spheres man is worked on by the
exalted beings of the first hierarchy, the Thrones,
Cherubim and Seraphim. He is also meeting those souls
with whom he is to have a connection in future lives on
Earth. Beyond this he goes out into the world of the fixed
stars, of the zodiac and the other constellations where,
Steiner tells us, he is worked on by 'influences pouring in
from infinitudes of spiritual worlds.' So immense are the
experiences which man goes through beyond death!

But now, having become entirely cosmic, having
reached a maximum of expansion, man has reached the
turning point of his existence between death and a new
birth. Now he is ready to begin his descent into earthly
human existence again, and so he sets out on the journey
back through all the planetary states through which he
came. But now, instead of laying aside qualities and faculties and impulses in order to advance to realms of pure
spirit, he receives from the beings of each of the planetary
realms gifts, capacities and faculties which he will employ
in his coming incarnation. So when we say that a person
appears on this Earth as a very gifted individual, that
expression is an exact one, for he has received gifts in the
course of his descent from the mighty beings of all the
nine hierarchies, from the Seraphim to the Angels.

Saturn gives the germ of the faculty of human memory.
Jupiter gives the faculty to conceive human thoughts.
Mars gives the spiritual substance out of which the
         human 'I' proceeds.

At the same time in these three spheres the spiritual
foundations of his future bodily structures are being laid.

When he enters the Sun sphere again, the first feelings
of his gradual separation from the cosmos begin to

appear. The heart in its spiritual aspect is formed here, at the heart of the universe, pulsating with the life of the beings of the second hierarchy who live in the Sun. In this realm, too, he makes the first connection with the hereditary stream in which, possibly centuries later, he will be born.

In the spheres of Venus and Mercury the shaping of his future destiny proceeds in relation to the particular family and particular nation to which he will later belong.

With the entry into the Moon sphere, decisive steps towards being born take place. Whereas on the way out beyond death a great expansion of consciousness took place in entering this sphere, now it is the task of spiritual beings to dim down man's consciousness to the level of the dream consciousness of a little child. This takes place during the same period in which the physical body for the incarnation is being prepared from conception to birth.

So the cycle from birth to death and from death to birth is completed.

O Death, fair Death, sole comforter and sweet,
Nor love nor hope can give such gifts as thine,
Sleep hardly shows us round thy shadowy shrine
What roses hang, what music floats, what feet
Pass and what wings of angels. We repeat
Wild words or mild, disastrous or divine,
Blind prayer, blind imprecation, seeing no sign
Nor hearing aught of thee not faint and fleet
As words of men or snowflakes on the wind,
But if we chide thee, saying, 'Thou hast sinned, thou
hast sinned,
Dark Death, to take so sweet a light away
As shone but late, though shadowed, in our skies.'
We hear thine answer — 'Night has given what day
Denied him: darkness hath unsealed his eyes.'

A.C. Swinburne

5 Help in Death

When Death lays his hand on a human being, there is a widespread tendency today to throw up our hands and say: 'There is nothing more we can do,' or when death has taken place, 'That is over. There is nothing to be done.' Such an attitude is a sign of the incapacity of our civilization to deal with the greatest experience of earthly life. Here the materialistic trend of human thought and the ignorance of man's true nature come most clearly to expression. And it is a completely unchristian attitude. Christianity stands or falls by the reality of the Resurrection: 'If Christ has not been raised then our preaching is in vain and your faith is in vain,' says St Paul (1Cor.15:14). And however little we may understand the resurrection of Christ, which is a mystery which transcends the capacities of purely intellectual thought (let alone materialistic thinking), it surely means at least this: that it belongs to a Christian view of death to believe that personality is not extinguished by death.

It follows then that there is still something we can do when death is approaching and after it has taken place. Medical science naturally concentrates attention on the physical body, and in a potentially fatal illness it is the daily symptoms of temperature, pulse and breathing which are most anxiously watched. Yet how easily does this cause the more subtle experiences which the soul of the patient is going through to be overlooked. The doctor and the nurse are all-important. If the minister or priest is sent for, then it is taken as a sign that all hope of recovery is given up. Yet it is not enough that, the priest is called in time to give the 'consolations of religion.' This is not the sum total of what he can, or should, do for a dying person. What is needed is a deeper understanding of this wonderful process of the release of the soul from the body — an understanding to be shared by relations, the nurse, the doctor, the priest and the patient himself. This may be a counsel of perfection — but if this book succeeds in contributing in some degree towards it, the writing of it will have been worth while.

What help then can the Christian religion give? In the first place it depends on what religion means to us throughout our life. Has it deepened and extended our awareness of a spiritual world with which we are deeply interwoven? Have we in fact found a connection to the being of Christ here on Earth?

In the practice of The Christian Community it is the Act of Consecration of Man, the restatement of the Sacrament of Bread and Wine as given through Rudolf Steiner, which is the central means to this end.* The receiving of this sacrament can be of the highest value to the soul in the last months or weeks of life, for it can assist in reorientating the soul towards the spiritual side of existence and away from the earthly. Further, it is a contact with that spiritual light of Christ, which is the means of unfolding the spiritual organs of the soul after death. In this connection it forms part of a bridge of light which spans the gulf of death.

The event of dying, the passing over into the spiritual world, is the greatest event of life. If we are planning to go abroad to another continent, to Africa, Australia or China, we make long and careful preparation for our journey. We 'read up' the country we are going to, study

---

* See E.F. Capel, *Seven Sacraments in The Christian Community.*

its language and customs. Yet for the greatest journey of
our lives we make, apparently, no preparation, although
we may suddenly and unexpectedly be called to make this
journey. I am not suggesting that we need to spend a lot
of our time thinking about dying (though there are
moments when we should). Our preparation should con-
sist in how we live, in our awareness of that other world
which is all around us but invisible, in recognizing the
spiritual in our lives. To this end we have the great help
of the sacraments, for through them we are in touch with
the invisible realities of existence.

The Act of Consecration of Man leads us from listening to the spirit-filled word to the act of offering in which,
turning away from our earthly pursuits and interests, we
approach the divine in an act in which also those who
have died can share. We unite our soul forces with Christ
and enter into a relation with the sphere of timeless existence which extends beyond death. Being in touch with
this realm we can also contact the souls of those who have
made the great transition before us, praying both for their
welfare and for their helping power towards us. But for
ourselves the whole process of the Act of Consecration of
Man is a purification, a preparation in which we antici-
pate, if only slightly, our eventual entry into the world of
spirit. In lifting up our souls to communion with Christ
we are laying up for ourselves treasure in heaven.

Much help, too, can be given by friends and relations
if they read with the person passages from the Bible (especially the Gospels) or other writings with a spiritual content. Very often devotional books which have been much
loved in earlier years are welcome (for instance, *The
Pilgrims' Progress, The Cloud of Unknowing,* Traherne's
Centuries of Meditations). Or, if the person is familiar
with Rudolf Steiner's works, then some lecture which has

meant much; but in any case what is both known and spiritually true. Experience shows how much reading or speaking about something of spiritual significance is appreciated by one who is seriously ill, rather than remarks about what the weather is like outside or other conventional chatter.

As life draws to an end, the tendency to look back on life becomes strong. Memories of youthful experiences become more vivid than what happened a few days ago. This is because the impressions we receive of the Earth while we are still incarnating leave a far deeper impression than those which surround us while we are gradually detaching ourselves from them. This is also a right tendency in preparation for the experiences after death, when we look back on the past life with a wider vision and a clearer judgment. For this reason we do something helpful and worthwhile when we listen with interest to an old person's reminiscences. They are very precious material to that person.

When the individual becomes aware of approaching death (which some people do quite a long time before it happens), it is good if he or she can make a deliberate and conscious review of the past life with the help of the priest, who will try to make clear its spiritual significance and bring to mind a kind of summing up of the earthly destiny. This culminates in the words spoken by the priest in the Sacramental Consultation,* which can bring peace to the soul as a preparation for the loosing of earthly connections and for a more intense turning towards the spiritual.

This conversation may then be followed by the reception of Communion, which can be administered at the

---

* See E.F. Capel, *Seven Sacraments in The Christian Community.*

bedside and can be shared in a more or less shortened form according to the condition and strength of the patient.

The last act of preparation, also of a sacramental character, is that of the Anointing. It can be said of this Sacrament that it is the spiritual counterpart of the natural fact of dying, just as the Sacrament of Baptism is the spiritual counterpart of the natural fact of being born. In both cases there is an inherent connection between the substances used and the processes taking place in the body of the individual concerned.

In a newly-born child, the child's soul, which has come out of the spiritual world, is engaged in taking possession of the bodily 'house' which is still being built. Three essential processes go on in the body in order that it can grow and live. There is the circulation of fluids — primarily the blood — with the heart as its central organ. This is represented by the substance water. There is the process of solidification and hardening, which builds the skeleton and hardens the skull and forms the teeth. This is like the forming of crystals in the earth and is represented by the substance salt. And thirdly there is the warmth process which works in the metabolic system and gives us a normal 'temperature.' This is represented by the substance ash, which is all that remains tangible when a burning process has taken place. So the substances which are sacramentally used correspond to the processes which make it possible for a soul to incarnate.

Now when a soul is in process of excarnation, something quite different takes place. If we think of a flowering plant which has reached its full development, the flower is fragrant and gives off a scent; think of a rose, or a violet, or lavender. In the petals of the flower are contained the so-called 'etheric' or essential oils, which vaporize and produce the scent. As they do so, the flower dies. So to the natural dying of a person we add, sacramentally, the substance oil (olive oil). Oils have a special quality of their own in that, when in a refined state, they tend to become volatile, that is, they want to fly away from the Earth. They tend to become 'spirit.' This is reflected even in the terms used for the material use of oils: refined petroleum oil becomes motor 'spirit'! Again a simple experiment, which anyone can make, of squeezing a piece of fresh orange peel close to a candle flame demonstrates this quality in the vegetable oils. In its nature oil has to do with passing over from one state to another. It is transitory. Sacramentally it has relationship to the passing on of the soul to a new state.

But there is another aspect of oil, which we should not overlook in regard to its sacramental use: that is its healing quality. The Good Samaritan applied oil and wine to heal the wounds of the man who fell among thieves, and most healing ointments have some vegetable oil as one of their constituents. The oil of the Anointing can be a factor in resolving an illness, whether it be towards recovery, or whether it be towards releasing the soul from the body. (This is, in a sense, also a 'healing.') We can never exclude the possibility of an unexpected rallying of forces in the mysterious psycho-physical processes of life and death. May not also our angel thereby be given a chance to intervene?

The Anointing is normally performed at the bedside in the presence of the intimate relatives and friends. The very brief act is preceded by the reading from the seventeenth chapter of St John's Gospel (the 'high-priestly prayer' of Christ to the Father). With the oil the priest makes a cross over each eye and in the middle of the forehead — three crosses on the place of the skull. This sign may call up for us the thought of the three crosses on Golgotha, from which, through the power of Christ, there sprang forth new life for humankind.

It is a good tradition that the room where a person is dying should be kept quiet and the light subdued. For when the soul is engaged in turning away from the earthly world and preparing to enter the spiritual world, it is only hindered in that work by strong sense impressions. These conditions can, of course, best be created in the home, which is the right place to die, just as it is the right place to be born. It is one of the penalties we pay for our modern 'civilization' that so much being-born and dying has to take place in hospitals. Essentially, hospitals are for the treatment of the sick. For that they are equipped. In the ideal case neither birth nor death need involve sickness, though it is clear that sickness may arise from the one and be the immediate cause of the other. But the institutional atmosphere of the hospital, the noise and bustle of a hospital ward, make it impossible to surround a dying person with the atmosphere of calm and spiritual thoughts which would be helpful. A nurse may do her best in this — but she has other duties on her mind. Relatives cannot be there constantly, and when they are, they are seldom at ease in the hospital atmosphere where they may feel themselves intruders.

The problem of surrounding the dying person with the right atmosphere is one which continues also after the last breath has been drawn. It is helpful at this time to surround the soul with a feeling of silent devotion. The connection of the soul with the body is still a very close one while the life-forces are gradually freeing themselves and the soul gazes on the life-panorama. A relative or friend on his own may read aloud from the Gospel of St John, but meditations for the dead should not be used until after the funeral.* Candles may be lighted in the room so that the body is not left in darkness but in a soft calm light. For royalty and other leading personalities there is held a 'lying in state,' and the picture of the royal coffin with the symbols of kingship laid on it, watched by the figures of officers of the forces standing motionless with bowed heads, as the people file past to pay their tribute, is a moving and unforgettable picture. If that is fitting for a king, should any human body be left uncared for and abandoned? Yet it happens often enough, because it is so widely held by people of today that once the heart stops beating the body becomes a corpse — and corpses are a matter for the 'authorities' to deal with! If death occurs in a hospital, the body is placed first in a mortuary chapel of the hospital until it can be removed by the undertaker. In most cases he has a small private chapel or room where, once the body has been prepared for burial and placed in the coffin, friends or relatives can, by arrangement with the undertaker, come in the day or two before the funeral.

As we have said, in normal circumstances it takes about three days for the life-forces to withdraw from the body, and it is clearly important that during this time the body should be disturbed as little as possible, so that the soul may contemplate the life-panorama without interruption. In cases of sudden or violent death, a post-mortem examination may be required by law in order to ascertain the cause of death. This interference with the body must be accepted as a part of earthly destiny.

We come now to the question of the form of burial and funeral service. Throughout human history great impor-

* See M. Jones, *Prayers and Graces,* p. 57ff.

tance has always been attached to the performance of proper religious ceremonies in connection with the disposal of the physical body. A right and decent burial, whether by interment or by burning, or, as with the Egyptians, by embalming, has always been regarded as indispensable to the welfare of the departing soul. We meet this thought in the Odyssey, when Odysseus visits the realm of Hades and, having made the offering of the blood of the sacrificed sheep, he speaks with the soul of his man Elpenor, who fell from the roof of Circe's palace and broke his neck. In their haste to leave the island, they left his body unburied on the shore. So Elpenor says to Odysseus: 'And now ... I beseech you, my prince, by all the absent friends we left behind, by your wife, by the father who supported you as a child, and by Telemachus, your only son, whom you left at home, by all these I beg you to remember me then and not to sail away and forsake me utterly nor leave me there unburied and unwept, or the gods may turn against you when they see my corpse. So burn me there with all my arms, such as they are, and raise a mound for me on the shore of the grey sea, in memory of an unlucky man, to mark the spot for future voyagers.'

From this we see that burial by cremation was practised by the Greeks, as also by the old Germanic tribes and in India. The Jews, on the other hand, buried their dead in graves and tombs.

One is often asked today: What are the arguments in favour of, or against, cremation as compared with interment in a grave?

On the practical level it is often pointed out that, with the growth of ever-larger urban areas, it is increasingly difficult to provide large enough cemeteries, and it is only the growth of the practice of cremation which has saved local authorities from an almost impossible problem. With this aspect, however, we are not here concerned.

What are the spiritual considerations? To make these clear, let us consider what happens when the body is burned and contrast with this the effect of embalming — a practice which is gaining considerable favour.

Cremation means a very rapid dissolution of the material parts of the body. In the high temperatures of a crematorium furnace the process takes only a few minutes. All that remains are the ashes, which are afterwards gathered up and placed in an urn, either to be preserved, or to be scattered in some place chosen by the deceased or his executors. The separation of the soul and spirit from the earthly element is made most complete by this means.

Embalming, on the contrary, preserves the body to the utmost extent and, as practised by the Egyptians of old, had the effect of affording a home to certain elemental spirits, who were the means whereby the priests of that time received communications from the spiritual world. For the soul, the body is still there and certain fine connections with it persist, so that the soul less easily frees itself from earthly ties to set out on its journey to the world of pure spirit.

Burial in the earth stands between the two in its effect for the soul. The destruction of the body is less rapid than by burning, but it is not preserved indefinitely. According to Rudolf Steiner, there is no difference in principle between burial and cremation, only in the time taken in the dissolution of the body. In either case the material parts of our physical body are given back to the element of earth. They become dust, 'and the dust returns to the earth as it was, and the spirit returns to God who gave it.' (Eccles.12:7) One qualification of the general principle has, however, to be made: where a person has led a very materialistic life or has committed suicide, then the sudden dissolution of the body by cremation could be a shock to the soul which, even after death, seeks the body still as the only thing on Earth with which he was strongly connected. In all other cases there is no objection, on spiritual grounds, to cremation, provided always that a full three days has elapsed since the death, during which time the soul should remain undisturbed in the contemplation of the life-panorama which has unfolded around it.

In The Christian Community the Burial Service is in two parts; the first is held at home, or if that cannot be, where the coffin has lain, preferably for the three days. It may also be held in the chapel. It is a very quiet, intimate act, conducted usually in the presence of only the nearest relatives and friends and, where possible, with the coffin open, so that the face of the dead is seen for the last time. People sometimes shrink from this experience, but if one has once seen the transfigured features of one who has died, when the stress and struggle of the illness is over and the face is calm and serene, one knows that great beauty can lie in this moment, supported as it is by the words of the ceremony which guide the thoughts of the bereaved to the realm of spirit which is now to be the home of the departing friend. At the conclusion the body is sprinkled with drops of consecrated water. May we not think of these as a reflection of the water of baptism at birth — or as a foreshadowing of a spiritual baptism of the soul in the other world?

The second, more public part, is held in the crematorium chapel or at the graveside though the graveside service is becoming the exception. The whole tone of the service, as indicated in the opening words, is one of accompanying and helping the departing soul with our thoughts and prayers. On the physical plane the material substances of the body are given back to the earth by dissolution into the elements of fire, air, water, earth. Spiritually we are concerned with the journey of the soul on into the world of soul and spirit. The holding of the Burial Service should correspond as nearly as possible in time with the moment when the soul experiences the 'awakening on the further shore' on the third or fourth day after death. We wish to support it in this transition to the world which is indeed its 'home,' but to which, through earthly life, it has become unaccustomed. A central concern in the service is that the eye of the soul may be opened in the world of soul and spirit. It is possible to go through death and be in the spiritual world and yet be blind, because the organ for perceiving it has not been developed. Whether this capacity is present or not, depends largely on how much interest we have taken in spiritual things on the Earth — not necessarily intellectually, but through our whole attitude to life in thinking, feeling and will, above all through our connection with Christ. For Christ is the great helper in death. Through his victory over death he has the power to light up for us the world beyond death. He is the giver of Light and Life, both in this world and the other. Therefore we pray that he may be with and in the one who is passing on. Consecrated water is sprinkled on the coffin, and incense is also burned, the outward token of our prayers ascending to the divine world. Though in many cases the ritual is strange and even puzzling to a number of those present, it is invariably felt to convey a reality, and this experience has been confirmed sometimes even by undertakers and crematorium attendants.

The last religious ceremony connected with death is the Memorial Act of Consecration, sometimes referred to as the Act of Consecration for the Dead. It is normally held on the Saturday following the funeral, and consists of the Act of Consecration of Man (the usual Communion Service) with a special prayer of intercession for the dead inserted near the end. The effectiveness of a prayer of intercession, whether in this or any other connection, depends on the degree of inner preparation which leads up to it. We need to adjust ourselves inwardly to the appropriate spiritual level. If we are to approach the being of God, the being of Christ, with a personal request (as we do in this service), it will be the more effective if we have already attuned ourselves to the divine, entered into the presence, before we venture to speak. That is why we first pass through the four stages of the service:

— the word of the Gospel to purify our minds;
— the Offertory to overcome our natural egotism with
    the power of love;
— the transmutation of the bread and the wine into
    bearers of Christ's own being into man's earthly life;
— the Communion as the receiving of the spiritual med-
    icine to overcome the sickness of sin.

Having thus made the inner ascent of 'the holy mountain,' our petition made in community, may be heard in the heavens above the clamour of earthly life. Relatives and friends may receive the Communion as an act of fellowship with the dead. That the dead are present and participate in such an act is the clear experience of all the priests who celebrate such an act, as also of those present. Where the soul concerned has lived with the Act of Consecration for many years, the experience is most powerful, but apart from that the reality of the ritual is one which reaches and has significance for the realm of the dead. Wherever there is spiritual light on Earth there is a point of contact between the dead and the living.

> What we bury deep
> In the grave to sleep
> Wrap of earth must be.
> What we love
> Abides above
> All through eternity.
> *Rudolf Steiner*

May my soul's love
Make its way unto thee:
May my love's inmost sense
Make its way unto thee:
That they sustain thee
That they enfold thee
In heights of hope
In realms of love.

Rudolf Steiner

6 Our Communion with the Dead

In the hour of bereavement many a person will cry out in despair at the sense of desolation, of loss, of separation, which the death of a beloved husband or wife, father or mother, brings to the one with whom there has been such a deep bond. One's whole view of the world is suddenly out of focus. The feeling can be overwhelming and may not be speedily overcome. Yet overcome it must be, both for the health and sanity of the one left on this side of the threshold, as also for the welfare and progress of the soul who has crossed it. Those left behind have to go on living, possibly under changed outer conditions as a result of the death, and have often to grapple immediately with new circumstances. Those who have passed on have, as we have seen in Chapter 4, very much to do and quite new conditions of existence to which to adapt. For these the grief of the others who wish them back again is a burden, is a drag on them in their efforts to get relaxed from earthly ties and to advance into the world of spirit. It is right for both that those left on Earth try to reach up to the sphere which holds the one who has gone, rather than to try in vain to pull him back. But our ability to do this depends on two things: firstly, our knowledge and understanding of the condition of life after death, and, secondly, our possessing the key to the technique of communion with the dead.

Let it first be said, that it is not morbid to seek communion with the dead, provided it is sought in the right way, that is, on a purely spiritual level. It is natural to seek it and it becomes the more natural as we get older and have more and more friends to think of in the other world. It arises from our life of prayer, for we cannot realistically speak of a 'prayer-life' if it does not include intercessory prayer both for the living and for the dead.

Let us consider therefore what we can do for the dead and what the dead can do for us. The condition of the dead is not such that they are in some far-off, remote place so that we have to send messages to them over immense distances, as we do today by the latest scientific devices to the moon and the nearer planets. And this is so, even when we say that they are in this or that planetary sphere, for they are no longer at points in space; they have spread themselves out in a process of expansion into the universe. They have achieved something of the quality of omnipresence, and, as in the Chinese play of 'Lady Precious Stream,' they are 'a thousand miles away and they are as near as breathing.' What separates us from them is only the veil of consciousness. So the first step towards our communion with them is to remember them, not only as living in the past, but as present with us now, in this room, at my shoulder as I write.

The memories we share in common with them are a bridge: we think of this or that particular occasion when we had a significant conversation with them, or shared in some difficult task with them — for the sharing of common sufferings and difficulties can be a strong uniting force, as can be experienced in many a hospital ward. The important thing is that they stand vividly before our mind's eye (that 'inner eye which is the bliss of solitude'). What have we done for them by this? We have opened a door for them. We have given them the possibility of having access to us, and that means that they can influence what happens on the Earth through us. For though the dead are concerned mainly with the forces of the cosmos, yet they have tasks in relation to the Earth which they cannot perform directly but only through us as intermediaries. Because we think so little about the dead, how frustrated they must feel when they want to send their helping forces to the Earth!

But beyond this, what can we do for them? During the years 1916 to 1918, Rudolf Steiner never began a lecture without first saying a meditation for the dead, and for those fighting in the war. The form of those meditations, as with others he gave, indicates how we may pray for the dead. They are an appeal to the spirit-guardians of human souls, that is to say their guardian angels, that the love offered by praying human hearts may be used for the help of the souls of the dead in conjunction with the wisdom and power which is wielded by the angels. The offering of the selfless love of human hearts is a force which we can place at the disposal of higher beings to be used in their discretion for the help of particular souls. By this means the egotism which so easily creeps into well-intentioned prayers — including the presumption of telling divine beings what we think should happen — is avoided. (This danger is all the greater in praying for the living.)

Now let us ask: How can the dead help us? What do the dead do for us? We not infrequently say: 'I have an idea!' and usually we feel pleased about it and think that it is very much to our credit to have had the idea. But where did it come from? The grey matter of our brain? 'It came into my mind,' we say. Yes, but who put it there? We cannot say 'we' did — it just came. If we were far more sensitive to the finer processes in our soul, if we were far more spiritually awake than we are, we might make the discovery that most of our 'bright ideas' are given us from

the other world, either by departed souls or by higher
beings. How much in life we should have to thank them
for, if we were but aware of their gifts!

This leads us to speak of a surprising principle regarding communication with the dead to which Rudolf Steiner
has drawn attention. There is a means whereby we may
put questions to a dead person and receive replies. This
can happen in the moment of going to sleep and the
moment of waking up, yet not at the level of waking consciousness. For at these moments we have meetings with
the dead, though these meetings are entirely in the realm
of our subconscious. It is only possible if we unite our life
of feeling with our thoughts and ideas.

Suppose a person has passed through the Gate of
Death and you want your subconscious to communicate
something in the evening. For it need not be communi-
cated consciously. You can prepare it at some time during
the day; then if you go to bed at ten o' clock at night having prepared it, say, at noon, it passes over to the dead
when you fall asleep. The question, however, must be put
in a particular way; it must not merely be a thought or an
idea, it must be imbued with feeling and will ... You must
remind yourself of your love for the dead when they was
alive and address yourself to them, not abstractly, but
with real warmth of heart. This can so take root in the
soul that in the evening at the moment of going to sleep
without your knowing it, it becomes a question to the
dead.* The answer then comes back to us at the moment
of waking — but what the dead say seems to arise out of
our own soul!

How very much more subtle, if also more difficult, is
this method of communication with the dead than the

* See Rudolf Steiner, *The Dead are with Us.*

methods of spiritualism. The desire to have physical sight of someone who has passed over, who may be able to give courage or confidence, or to hear his voice, is one which has been fairly widespread right through the ages. Saul went to the Witch of Endor (to a medium) and ordered her to call up the spirit of Samuel. But the first thing that Samuel said was: 'Why have you disturbed me by bringing me up?' That is the justified rebuke whenever a soul on the other side is forced into some physical or sense-perceptible manifestation through the agency of a medium. For the dead it is an unwarranted intrusion into their existence and drags them back into Earth conditions to satisfy the desire of those on Earth.

There also exists the great danger that, when contact is ostensibly made with some known individuality, what then speaks is not in fact the 'I,' the spirit of that person. In the progress of the soul after death, described previously, it discards successively various wrappings or sheaths. The etheric life-body dissolves after three to four days into the elemental world, yet sufficient of it remains together to constitute an 'etheric corpse.' This etheric corpse can be animated and used by those who are called elemental spirits to produce an illusion of the personality who has abandoned these wrappings and gone on. These elemental spirits are clever and just because they cannot themselves incarnate physically, take a delight in imitating an individual and, through the remnants of his etheric body, they can mimic his habits, movements, mannerisms and way of speaking. All this is a great trap for those who seek contact with the other world through mediums. The possibilities of illusions and deceptions, even for the honest seeker, are very great.

The importance of our communion with the dead on a purely spiritual basis cannot be emphasized sufficiently.

It far outweighs the value of communication with the dead which, when sought, all too often centres on trivialities. Nowhere can we better or more safely and healthily foster our communion with the dead than when we worship at the altar, a place which, both in symbol (for the altar is shaped like a tomb) and in reality, is a threshold between the visible and the invisible worlds. Here, whenever we celebrate the renewed form of the altar sacrament, we twice invoke the participation of the dead. They form one of the three circles of community with whom we 'bring the offering': those present, all true Christians who are born, those who have died. And we pray that the burden of their temporal, earthly nature may not overwhelm their eternal part and bind it to the Earth. Even if no congregation is physically present, the congregation of the dead is always there to take part. In the second place we invoke the sheltering power of those who have gone before us, having found the Christ-Spirit within them.

That they exercise a sheltering power comes to expression in an experience which many a person has had when he or she is held back, 'by chance,' as it seems, from going to some place where they would certainly have been killed. An unexpected caller delays them and causes them to miss a train which is involved in a serious smash. In wartime many a person has had an impulse to go to another room to fetch a book, or to see if the window is shut, just in time to escape being killed by a bomb which demolishes the place he has just left. The feeling: I was lucky that time, is common in such circumstances. More rarely does the thought come: Who or what prompted me to fetch the book or see to the window? Here is no 'chance,' but the working of some influence from the invisible world.

It is of the highest importance, not only for ourselves, but for the Earth and its affairs, that we should cultivate a sensitivity for the invisible world, a world to which we retire when we sleep, a world from which we come when we enter on the 'brief span of life,' a world in which we shall spend a far greater time after death. The universe is one, and we are citizens of the whole of it, whether in life or in death.

Wert thou some Starr which from the ruin'd roofe
Of shak't Olympus by mischance did fall;
Which carefull Jove in nature's true behoofe
Took up, and in fit place did reinstall?
Or did of late Earth's Sonnes besiege the wall
Of sheenie Heav'n, and thou some goddess fled
Amongst us here below to hide thy nectar'd head?

Or wert thou that just Maid who once before
Forsook the hated earth, O tell me sooth,
And cam'st again to visit us once more?
Or wert thou that sweet-smiling Youth?
Or that crown'd Matron, sage white-robèd Truth?
Or any other of that heav'nly brood
Let down in clowdie throne to do the world some good?

Or wert thou of the golden-winged host,
Who having clad thyself in human weed,
To earth from thy prefixed seat didst post,
And after short abode fly back with speed,
As if to show what creatures Heav'n doth breed,
Thereby to set the hearts of men on fire
To scorn the sordid world, and unto Heav'n aspire?

John Milton, 'On the Death of a Fair Infant'

Whom the gods love die young.

Menander

7 Premature Death and Suicide

The death of a child

When a child dies, an urgent questioning arises in the hearts of parents, relatives and friends: Why must this happen? With the death of an old person we may also feel great sadness and sense of loss, yet we recognize the inevitability of death and the questions in our minds concern the 'when' rather than the 'why.' But with a child, when so many hopes for the future are shattered by untimely death, when so many unfolding capacities and talents are nipped in the bud, we feel we have to ask: How does this make sense? Is it just? Is it fair? Feelings of bitterness can mingle with grief: 'What have I done that God should take away this young life?' Many a mother has asked herself: Is this punishment for sins I have committed? — Terrible self-recrimination and remorse may arise in such circumstances. But the causes do not lie in such a personal human element. Nor do the times of birth and death lie in the realm of human decision. Here the angels, out of their higher wisdom, take a hand in human affairs.

The child's soul has sought the Earth in order to gain experiences of value to it. Its withdrawal, therefore, amounts to a disappointment, a frustration of its impulse. It longs to be on the Earth, for, as we have already described, it has been preparing this incarnation over long periods of time. It therefore suffers because it has had to withdraw from the physical body. The parents suffer from the pain of losing the child on whom they had set great hopes. The sorrow of parents and child is therefore mutual and, because it is shared, there is an element of comfort for both. Yet its brief visit may have given it at least the feeling of the great love of the parents, and also the experiences of Christian baptism, which, in some circumstances, might in itself be a reason for coming to the Earth.

When it goes back into the spiritual world, it does not withdraw from the Earth in the same way or to the same extent that an older person does. It seeks experience through the parents and their feelings are therefore important to it. It lives in intimate connection with them and spiritually they do not lose the child. As it had not reached 'earthly maturity' (that is, the age of puberty), it does not have to go through the long period of purification which is the consequence of a full span of life. It has not crossed the threshold from Innocence to Experience. This we might compare to a 'point of no return,' as with a plane flying across an ocean. Up till the fourteenth or fifteenth year the soul can still draw back from full incarnation; it is not irrevocably committed. Some critical illnesses at this age may be connected with the attempt to draw back. After the changes in the relationship of soul and body, which we call puberty, have taken place, then, as Wordsworth puts it, 'shades of the prison house begin to close upon the growing boy' and there is no option but to go on. The door of childhood has closed and the full consequences of an earthly incarnation ensue.

This is why there is in The Christian Community a form of Burial Service for children which is radically different in content and mood from that which is used for adults. We do not have to accompany the soul of a child on a path of withdrawal into the world of spirit. Our thoughts are much more concerned with the grief which is felt here on Earth, a grief with which is associated a strong element of compassion. This is quite different from the grief which we feel at the loss of an older person, which is a feeling more egotistical in its nature and which we have to overcome through lifting ourselves up to the realm of the dead. The child has not gone on — it has rather stepped back into the world of pre-birth, and there, where the soul's impulses are directed earthward, it continues ever present with us. It stays with us spiritually.

Stillbirth and cot death

For a woman to give birth to a child is one of the greatest achievements of her life and therefore if the child is born dead, this is both a great tragedy and an experience of shock which is very difficult to get over. The mother may find it important to have at least once held the dead infant in their arms, and this is a delicate matter which must be approached gently. It is equally important for those attending a case of stillbirth to recognize that a birth has taken place. Though modern hospital practice is now generally sensitive to this point, it would be quite wrong if medical staff or relatives treat the birth as a non-event when it is a shattering experience for the mother. For her the child is real, has been part of her life for months. A tentative name may even be in the parents' minds. If they wish, a burial should take place with suitable prayers and readings of comfort and beauty.

A distinction must be made here between a stillbirth where the pregnancy has run its full term and what at an earlier stage would be a miscarriage. Depending on the stage of pregnancy, the disposal of the foetus may be the responsibility of the hospital. In this case the parents may wish to attend an Act of Consecration in special memory of the soul that has drawn near to them.

In a cot death, or in any case where the child has drawn breath, the child should have a full burial service. In the case of a stillbirth, the advice of the local priest or minister should be sought.

But what lies behind these two phenomena? One thing must be clear: no blame attaches to the mother. What has happened belongs to the destiny of the incarnating soul. One has to ask: what has been the purpose of this all too brief incarnation? Has this soul achieved something through this slight contact with Earth existence? Has it given the soul something it lacked? Or, on the other hand, has the advent of this soul contributed a valuable, if painful, experience to the lives of parents, nurses and others who have had to do with it? The smallest infant can exert an influence on its surroundings.

Premature death

Those who die young, having left childhood behind, but still possessing the enthusiasms and ideals of youth, leave us with a particular poignancy of memory. It is natural to think in such cases of the loss to the world of the contribution which such young men and women might have made, had they lived. Is there not here a senseless waste of human talents?

We must oppose to this thought the idea that in the economy of God — which is not the economy of this world — there is no waste. Those who are 'withdrawn from circulation' in this world are required either for other tasks in the spiritual world or for future tasks on Earth. For the divine Providence does not work on a day-to-day basis but in terms of centuries and millennia. So the preparation of some event centuries ahead may require the return of some souls to the spiritual world now. May we not regard the genealogy of Christ at the beginning of St Matthew's Gospel not only as a linking passage between the Old and New Testaments, but also as a suggestion that the lives of all those generations of individuals had their meaning and purpose, though all unconsciously, in preparing for the incarnation of Christ?

The unfulfilled ideals of those who die in the first half of life can become effective forces in the spiritual world for the starting of new impulses, new movements on the Earth. They are sources of spiritual inspiration. We cannot deny that wars are the most tragic form of stupidity that can befall humankind, and they occur largely because human minds are so closed to the inspiration which can come from the other world. But through the very lives which are sacrificed, the aims of the spirit do sometimes break through into our civilization, although this progress is purchased at the price of bloodshed. Those who die young are 'beloved of God' in the sense that they are specially needed to prepare the future of humankind. We may therefore give thanks for their promotion to higher worlds.

Suicide

To take one's own life, to do away with oneself, has generally been recognized as a wrong and for many centuries treated as a crime in many parts of the civilized world. Spiritually, the individual who does this abrogates a right which belongs to higher spiritual beings. For the hour in which we die is part of our destiny and is determined not merely out of causes to be found in this world. With some people one has the impression that only when their life-task was completed could such a person die. With others, though their life work was ended, they had to wait for a certain moment when they could be recalled to the world of the planets and the stars. Just as we are born under a certain constellation, so it lies in our destiny to die under a certain constellation. So to take one's own life is to interfere with the operation of one's destiny.

The usual verdict of a coroner's court is: 'Suicide while of unsound mind,' and this verdict expresses the common view that no person in their right mind would commit suicide. What, then, leads apparently sensible people to kill themselves? It might be thought that when circumstances become oppressive, through war, famine or poverty, the inclination to commit suicide increases. But statistics do not on the whole support this idea. When war breaks out the nation braces itself for a great effort. We are all in it together, is the mood. The sense of common destiny, of community, is strengthened and the suicide rate falls. Again one might think that the dark and gloomy months of the year, November and December, would show an increased number of suicides. In fact, the highest figures occur in April and May, when spring is here and the world of nature is at its most beautiful. But it is just in that season that depressions and restlessness of soul are most common.

All this points to the fact that the causes lie less in outer circumstances than in inner conflicts. It is these which disturb the balance of mind and admit the destructive forces. They are most dangerous when they are repressed and not allowed to come to expression. The difficulty must be talked out, either with a trusted friend — and there is probably no greater safeguard against suicide than to have a trusted friend — or with a minister or priest. This is the good aspect of the Catholic practice of Confession, which is replaced in The Christian Community by the freely sought Sacramental Consultation. It is held by some people that suicide is less common in Catholic than in Protestant countries because of this practice, and there may be an element of truth in this, but because a number of others factors play in as well — climate, national temperament, social tradition — statistics do not clearly prove this.

The inner condition which tends most strongly towards suicide is that in which life appears to have no meaning and no purpose. Unemployment is an external factor which contributes to this, not so much because of hardship — the welfare state largely mitigates that — but from the meaninglessness of life, because to have a job, to work in whatever form, is felt to be necessary to the dignity of a human being. To survive years of unemployment without falling into a state of demoralization demands an inner strength and resourcefulness which not every person has. In this connection it may be seen as significant that in the United States the suicide rate, analysed by age groups, shows a steady rise with advancing years, with a peak at the sixty-fourth to seventy-fourth year period which corresponds with the age of retirement for a man.

The need to find a satisfying activity for the years of retirement, which can give a continuing sense of purpose after business or professional activity has ceased, is the crux of the problem. Very often the answer is to be found in hobbies or cultural activities (painting, music and so on) for which an interest already exists. Above all, interest in spiritual things is important at this stage.

But apart from old age, to find life meaningless at any age is a dangerous condition. It is a tragedy of our time that so many people — and young people in particular — find no meaning in life, no purpose which makes it worth while to struggle to overcome oppositions; this leads them to seek what pleasurable sensations they can find in drink or drugs or sex and, when these fail them, there is no reason to go on existing without meaning, and destructive impulses take possession of the shell of the soul. These may at first be turned outward in acts of violence against society but in the last resort against the self in suicide.

Apart from these cases one is sometimes surprised and shocked at the suicide of highly intelligent people who have every means of knowing the implications of their act — and yet do it. One sees from such cases that, when it comes to the point, it is usually an irrational impulsive act, springing out of the mood at the moment, an impulse of will not controlled by the head.

The fate of such a soul after death is tragic indeed. First, there is the waking to the fact that death does not end all — which is always part of the illusion of the suicide. Then the discovery that, far from having freed oneself from the Earth by this act, one has in fact bound one's soul nature more closely to it and feels the longing to be reunited with the body one has so rashly destroyed.

Acts of suicide vary in quality and meaning. A student

who hangs himself commits a different kind of act from the terminally ill person who takes an overdose of sleeping pills. The former deprives himself of a lifetime of experiences, while the latter anticipates the inevitable outcome of his illness. Not that one should regard that as a justification but that one may judge the significance of the act differently. Chronic depression can be a serious and dangerous illness which drives some people to commit suicide. Such people are in great need of help to overcome their inner loneliness.

This leads on to the much debated question of euthanasia. The arguments are based on the one hand on compassion and on the desire to relieve excessive suffering, and on the other on the conviction that it is wrong to give any person the right or duty of taking away another person's life. One may also say from a religious point of view that life is the gift of God, and God alone should determine when it should end. One can have great sympathy with anyone who has to watch a loved one suffer over a long period of time and no-one wishes to appear callous towards such a situation, but to legislate for all the changes of circumstance and mood in illness, whatever their views in theory may be, is all but impossible. If I decide today, being in good health, that if I should develop cancer and be in extreme pain and authorize a doctor to terminate my life and if in three months time I develop the illness and find a therapy which makes it at least tolerable, will not my instinct to cling to life prevail?

Looked at from a spiritual understanding of destiny one would have to say that in the spiritual world before birth we have been guided by our angel, been given a glimpse of our coming earthly destiny and out of that higher state of consciousness have said Yes to it, with all the suffering it may involve, because it seems the right

and necessary thing for our spiritual progress. In this pre-
view is also included the moment of death, which is also
part of destiny and not arbitrary or mere chance.
Euthanasia is then an interference with that destiny
which, while we are on Earth, we cannot see in its whole-
ness, but for which the spiritual world will give help in
proportion to the courage we develop in meeting it. The
process of purifying the soul in order to find oneself as
spirit among spirits is far longer and more painful in such
a case, and, moreover, the capacity of the soul to perceive
the light which streams from the beings of the hierarchies
is impaired, so that spiritual darkness is experienced on
top of other miseries. There is, therefore, desperate need
to pray for such a soul. An intensive 'barrage of prayer' (if
this clumsy metaphor be allowed) is one means whereby
we can help such a straying soul to find itself.

Dr Moody in his second book, *Reflections on Life after
Life* reports that of those people he has interviewed in
regard to their 'near death' experiences resulting from
attempted suicide, none now sees this as a solution to the
difficulties of life. One man said he had the impression
that there was a 'penalty' to pay for some acts of suicide
and that part of this would be to witness the suffering on
the part of others which this act would cause.

The old practice of refusing Christian burial to suicides
was against the spirit of compassion of true Christianity.
They are judged for their deeds by the laws of the spiritual world and need no condemnation by Christians on
the Earth. 'Let him who is without sin among you first
cast a stone.' Rather pray for those who are in danger that
they may be defended by their guardian angel against the
temptation to self-destruction and pray for those who
have taken this tragic step that the light of Christ may
lighten their darkness.

I hold that when a person dies
His soul returns again to earth;
Arrayed in some new flesh-disguise
Another mother gives him birth.
With sturdier limbs and brighter brain
The old soul takes the road again.

Such is my own belief and trust;
This hand, this hand that holds the pen,
Has many a hundred times been dust
And turned, as dust, to dust again;
These eyes of mine have blinked and shone
In Thebes, in Troy, in Babylon.

All that I rightly think or do,
Or make, or spoil, or bless, or blast,
Is curse or blessing justly due
For sloth or effort in the past.
My life's a statement of the sum
Of vice indulged or overcome.

...

So shall I fight, so shall I tread,
In this long war beneath the stars;
So shall a glory wreath my head,
So shall I faint and show the scars,
Until this case, this clogging mould,
Be smithied all to kingly gold.

John Masefield, A Creed

8 Reincarnation and Destiny

Reincarnation is a controversial subject and arouses strong feelings in some people. Though it is rejected as 'unchristian' by many Church people, in recent years a greater readiness to consider it as a possible explanation of some of the riddles of life has become apparent. Yet it is an ancient idea. If you start to look up the history of the subject, you will find the notion of *metempsychosis* leading back to Pythagoras and the doctrine of the Transmigration of Souls, that is, that human souls after death can go over into the bodies of animals, or may have come from them or even from plants. In a passage from Empedocles we find:

> For I was once already boy and girl,
> Thicket and bird, and mute fish in the waves.
> All things doth Nature change, enwrapping souls
> In unfamiliar tunics of the flesh.

But not all the Greek thinkers agreed with this far-reaching view. Thus Hierocles, commenting on Pythagoras says:

> He who believes that he transmigrates after death into the body of a beast or plant is grossly mistaken; he is ignorant of the fact that the essential form of the human soul cannot change, that it is and it remains human, and only metaphorically speaking does virtue make it a god and vice an animal.

Shakespeare refers more than once to this belief. For example in *Twelfth Night:*

CLOWN: What is the opinion of Pythagoras concerning wild fowl?
MALVOLIO: That the soul of our grandam may inhabit a bird.
CLOWN: What thinkest thou of his opinion?
MALVOLIO: I think nobly of the soul and no way approve his opinion.

Other witnesses cited by the *Encyclopedia Britannica* for the belief are: Plato, Menander, the Jewish Cabbalists, the Manicheans, the Cathars, and the Theosophists.

But is an acceptance of the fact of reincarnation compatible with Christian belief? First, it must be stated that, if we turn to the Bible, we find neither proof nor convincing refutation of the idea. At the most one can say that the idea was not entirely unfamiliar in Palestine at the time of Christ. The passages usually quoted in support of this are: 'and if you are willing to accept it, he [John] is Elijah who is to come. He who has ears to hear, let him hear.' (Matt.11:14f). This was Christ's testimony concerning John the Baptist which he gave to the multitude after John had sent disciples to ask: 'Are you he who is to come?' As to whether they accepted it or not, they were left free. The same theme recurs in Matthew when as the three disciples descend the mountain with Jesus after the Transfiguration, they ask him: ' "Then why do the scribes say that first Elijah must come?" He replied, "... Elijah has already come, and they did not know him [i.e. John was not recognized as the reincarnated Elijah], but did to him whatever they pleased. So also the Son of man will suffer at their hands." Then the disciples understood that he was speaking to them of John the Baptist.' (17:10–13) It might be argued that this was a special and exceptional case, but even if that be granted, it admits in principle the possibility of reincarnation, and therefore the probability of others having the experience is at least not excluded.

Nor does the denial by John himself: 'I am not,' when asked: 'Are you Elijah?' (John 1:21), do more than suggest that he was not himself aware of his previous life, at least on the level of ordinary human consciousness. On the other hand John was no ordinary man ('of all those born of women none is greater than John') and in higher states of consciousness he may indeed have known of his previous life, but out of the selflessness of his nature did not wish to be known other than as the 'voice crying in the wilderness,' or as the Baptist. Normally, however, even those who believe in reincarnation can only in rare cases remember their previous lives.

Then the question of the disciples concerning the man born blind: 'Master, who did sin, this man or his parents, that he was born blind?' (John 9:2) can at the most be held to show that the disciples were not unfamiliar with the thought that limitations in this life might be caused by sins in a previous one. It certainly cannot be said to prove a doctrine of reincarnation, especially as Christ then negates both suggestions, not because they were inherently false — that the sins of the fathers were visited on the children was sound Jewish doctrine — but because their approach to the question was wrong. Christ was looking to the future, not to the past. Not the 'why?' but 'to what end?' is important. It does, however, seem reasonable to think that the idea of reincarnation was neither unknown nor unusual at the time of Christ. Summing up the evidence of Scripture, one can only say that it is inconclusive, but does not exclude the idea. Dr Leslie

Weatherhead, in a stimulating little booklet *(The Case for Reincarnation)* states: 'Some have felt that a belief in reincarnation is not compatible with Christian orthodoxy. If this could be substantiated, it would be a formidable indictment, but, in my opinion, it cannot.'

Why then did the idea of reincarnation, which was current in the pre-Christian era and is generally implicit in most Eastern teaching, have to disappear — with few exceptions — from the whole development of exoteric Christianity hitherto? (Knowledge of it was always preserved in esoteric circles.) Why does it come up again now?

One can say that it had to die and be born again in a new form because of the evolution of man through a period of materialism. Man had to develop a predominantly earthly consciousness, to find himself as an individual on the Earth, to pass through the Age of Faith, the Age of Discovery, the Age of Reason, the Age of Science, to emerge into a new Age of Spiritual Knowledge and understanding. To the establishment of this new Age, Rudolf Steiner has made contributions unique both in their content and variety. One of them is the investigation of the working of the law of destiny and reincarnation. Friedrich Rittelmeyer, the first leader of The Christian Community, records that, in his first conversation with Rudolf Steiner, he raised the question of reincarnation and Christianity, to which Rudolf Steiner replied: 'Reincarnation is not a doctrine of Christianity, but it is a result of investigation with which Christianity must reckon.'

That the idea of reincarnation has its dangers must be readily admitted. It provides material for the most fantastic speculations and immense egotism. Both inside and outside of the mental hospitals are countless people who believe themselves to be reincarnations of Napoleon, Shakespeare, Helen of Troy, Socrates, and other famous people. Such ideas are shadows cast by the new light. All truth can be perverted, and in some disturbed souls the practice of religion can turn to religious mania. Nor can some of the vague feelings of 'having been here before' or 'all this has happened before,' which many people have, be considered as evidence of previous lives. There are many slightly unusual experiences possible to the human soul, such as 'second sight,' which have nothing what ever to do with reincarnation. Yet there are numbers of people who have had memories or visions of previous lives which cannot so easily be dismissed in this category.*

The fact that most of us do not remember our previous lives is no more evidence against the truth of reincarnation, than the fact that we have no memory of our experiences in sleep is evidence that our soul and 'I' do not go into spiritual spheres with angels and other spiritual beings, who enable us to return refreshed into our body when we wake.

But if we are prepared to accept the idea of repeated Earth lives and that the researches of spiritual science can tell us more about this idea — how does it work? We have indicated, in our attempt to describe the passage of the human spirit beyond death and on to new birth, how we must first lay aside all the impulses, longings and wishes connected with our past earth-life in order to become akin to the highest spirit-beings, and how we then in our descent receive from them the spiritual gifts — the spiritual equipment, we might call it — for our next life. But there are also those impulses to make good, to make compensation for

* See, for instance, recent research in this area in *Thinking beyond the Brain,* ed. David Lorimer.

what went wrong last time, which arise in us during the period of purification, but which have to wait for their fulfilment until we a again have an earthly body which we can use as an instrument. When we enter the Moon sphere before birth, we take up again the account book of our destiny. We read in it the entries to our debit and credit. We see the liabilities arising from our previous life, which we shall have to meet; we know that we are equipped with certain assets. We cannot know whether, when we come to pay a certain debt, we shall have realized sufficient of our assets to pay it in full. Our assets are of a spiritual kind; the extent to which we convert them into earthly currency is something which falls within the realm of human freedom. In some such way we may picture to ourselves the nature of human destiny.

The question of how one reconciles destiny and free will is one of the most constantly recurring themes in our Christian Community discussion groups. We cannot deal with it at length here, but let us select one aspect: the horoscope. Popular astrology has a fascination for many thousands of modern people, most of whom are largely sceptical about it, but yet 'feel there is something in it.' Their intellect says: 'Of course it is all rubbish, really.' But their heart says, 'But all the same I am connected with the stars,' and mostly the heart wins, and they read some astrological books or journals. The head is right to be sceptical of the popular presentation; the heart is right to feel that there is a spiritual truth underlying it. For what is the birth horoscope? It records the time by the stars when we first drew breath, and the configuration of our soul is the result of the working of star forces (that means, the influences of spiritual beings whose symbol or emblem the constellations are) which have carefully prepared us to enter the world at that particular moment. We have, as it were, 'clocked in' for our earthly work at that hour by the cosmic clock. The horoscope is our duly stamped time-card! It certifies that certain influences, impulses, capacities are implanted in us. From these data some deductions can be made as to our character, some forecast made of the probable course of our life. But, like a weather forecast, it is not one hundred per cent certain that it will be true in all circumstances. That approaching depression may change its course and pass a hundred miles further north! That is the glorious privilege of living on the Earth: that out of our freedom we can change our course. That is why the picture of a ship has so often and so appropriately been used as an image for human destiny. We sail in a certain ship, having certain equipment. We set out from a certain port on a certain course and are subject to certain prevailing winds, currents and tides. But we ourselves steer the ship, wisely or badly, for good or ill and can change its course. We are not predestined to go on the rocks. By wise navigation we can come safely by. There is one star that holds us true to our course: that is Christ.

It is often asked: At what intervals of time do we return to the Earth? The answers which spiritual science gives indicate that between individual cases there are great variations. Some individualities return much sooner than others; some remain longer in the spiritual world. But in principle it is linked with the fact that we come to the Earth each time to have new experiences. Therefore we wait for a new incarnation till conditions on the Earth have quite changed. This has taken place fully — from a spiritual point of view — when the sun, at its spring rising point, has moved through one constellation (one-twelfth) of the zodiac. This takes about 2160 years. But

because our incarnations normally (but not always) alter-
nate between a male and a female incarnation and the
experience of living as a man and living as a woman is so
different, we come back to sufficiently changed conditions after a 'normal' interval of about a thousand years.
That is to say that many people living today may only
have experienced one previous Christian incarnation,
since the preceding one would, on this principle, have
taken place some years before Christ. But, as we have seen
in speaking of early death, there are souls who, for special
reasons in their destiny, may be recalled early to the spiritual world in order to prepare for another earth-life after
only a short interval, because they are required to play a
part in world events at that time. We should, therefore,
avoid having too rigid a concept of the time which elapses
between one earth-life and the next.

What do we gain from this knowledge of reincarnation? Amongst other things, it provides an answer to
many a question about the apparent injustices of life. Why
are some born 'with a silver spoon in their mouth,' while
others have a hard time all through life? Why are some
people clever, gifted, geniuses even, while others are dull,
stupid or backward? All these conditions have their causes
in previous lives, though that does not mean that our
present gifts are the same ones which we had, or developed, last time. They have undergone a metamorphosis.
Moreover we seek not the same, but rather the opposite
kind of experiences to those we previously had. If in one
life we have carried power and public responsibility, we
may seek in the next a life of humble obscurity. Those
who are 'nobodies' today, may be husbanding their spiritual potentialities to be 'somebodies' in the future. All are
souls in the making. For each one the experience of Earth
is vitally important, even if it brings sorrow and suffering

— yes, even for the mentally or physically handicapped from birth. They call forth selfless love from those who tend them. They educate their educators. They may not do much, in a worldly sense, but that they are there is an important social and spiritual fact.

For the moral conduct of our life on Earth, a great deal depends on what we regard as the meaning and purpose of life. If we see it *only* as a series of troubles, pains and sufferings, then we shall naturally feel that to come back and go through it all again is more than we can bear. Then we may fall back with the eastern Buddhist view that the aim of life is to gain release from the wheel of return. But the distinctive element in Christian thinking springs from the fact that Christ united himself with the Earth and remains united with it. Therefore, if we are followers of Christ, our Earth is the most important place to be whether we experience suffering there or not. It is the place where we can in freedom place ourselves in his service and where we can be fruitful.

An apple tree is fulfilling its purpose when it stands with its branches laden with fruit. In order to be fruitful, it has to 'die' when its season is over and to gather into its sap new forces for the following year. If the tree could speak and say: 'It is a great burden to have to bear so much fruit: I prefer not to have leaves and blossom and fruit next year' — it would have no purpose. It fulfils its purpose as an apple tree if it produces more and better fruit year by year.

So for us the opportunity of returning to earthly incarnation enables us to fulfil more perfectly our purpose as human beings; yet only more perfectly in so far as we make efforts to develop ourselves morally and spiritually. In this sense, therefore, reincarnation encourages a feeling of responsibility in our moral and spiritual life. If, too, we reflect that our life-span of sixty, seventy or eighty years is very short in relation to the time we spend in the spiritual world between incarnations, we may become aware how precious each single day is, in that it gives opportunity to do something for the good of others, or at least to think some good thoughts, or to wrestle with some fault or weakness in ourselves.

Sleep sleep old Sun, thou canst not have repassed
As yet, the wound thou took'st on Friday last;
Sleep then, and rest; Thy world may bear thy stay,
A better Sun rose before thee today,
Who, not content to enlighten all that dwell
On the earth's face, as thou, enlightened hell,
And made the dark fires languish in that vale,
As at thy presence here our fires grow pale.
Whose body having walked on earth, and now
Hasting to Heaven, would, that He might allow
Himself unto all stations, and fill all,
For these three days become a mineral;
He was all gold when He lay down, but rose
All tincture, and doth not alone dispose
Leaden and iron wills to good, but is
Of power to make even sinful flesh like His.

John Donne, 'Resurrection'

Then he overcame death after three days.

The Creed of The Christian Community

9 The Vanquisher of Death

In all forms of the Christian Creed, whether it be the Apostles' Creed, the Nicene Creed or the formulation of the Creed as used in the Act of Consecration of Man, it may be noticed that nothing is said of the three years of Christ's earthly ministry, nothing of his teaching, his healings, his miracles, his temptation or transfiguration. A jump is made from 'born of the Virgin Mary' to 'suffered under Pontius Pilate,' from his incarnation to his death. One may think this is just for the sake of brevity, but, on the other hand, it may be interpreted as emphasizing that the most important thing which Christ achieved on the Earth was his death.

This is indeed true and is that which distinguishes Christianity from all other religions. Christ's death was not just a human tragedy, but a unique fact in the history of the Earth. The gods do not know death. No being of the celestial hierarchies experiences it — only man. So for the divine Christ-being to descend to the Earth, to take upon him the form of a man, and to go through death was a cosmic event of tremendous significance. No wonder that the earth quaked and trembled, that the sun hid its face and the veil of the Temple was rent when the God died upon the cross!

The consequences of this are much more radical and far reaching than we generally think or recognize. What would have happened to the Earth and to us if Christ had not died, overcome death and risen from the dead? Rudolf Steiner answers this question in the following terms.

... about the time of the Mystery of Golgotha the human physical body had reached a degree of decline where the men who were then in incarnation or who were to be incarnated in the near future, that is up to about the fourth century AD, were faced with the danger of leaving an Earth that was growing more and more desolate and barren, and of finding no possibility in the future of descending from the world of spirit-and-soul and building a physical body out of materials provided by the physical earth. This danger existed, and the inevitable consequence would have been the failure of man to fulfil his allotted earthly mission.
('Supersensible Man,' lecture of May 7, 1923.)

In other words, I might not have been here to write this book, nor you to read it!

It is important to recognize that the 'redemption by Christ' means not merely the redemption of man's moral and spiritual nature, but also the redemption of his physical and etheric nature — that is; the saving of it from the destructive influences which have worked in Man's body through the hereditary forces since the power of Lucifer brought about Man's Fall. Therefore, St Paul says: 'As in Adam all die, even so in Christ shall all be made alive,' and in the Creed, as used in The Christian Community, we say: '... who, to heal spiritually the sickness of sin of the bodily nature of mankind, prepared the son of Mary to be the vehicle of the Christ.' Both for the Earth as a living organism and for Man in his total nature, the death and resurrection of Christ represented an injection of new life.

Yet if Christ overcame death, how is it that man still experiences death and can still feel its terror? To die is a condition of our earthly existence and is, as I have tried to show, but a gateway leading from this state of existence to another. It is that other state of existence which has also undergone a transformation through Christ.

Christian tradition asserts that, in the time between his death on the cross and his resurrection on Easter morning, Christ 'descended into hell,' into that realm which the Jews called 'Sheol' and the Greeks 'Hades,' the kingdom of the shades, in which all souls before Christ had to dwell in a lonely and shadowy state. A vivid description of this is to be found in Homer's *Odyssey*. From this condition, which was not a punishment for the wicked but an unavoidable experience for pre-Christian souls, Christ rescued humankind. There is a beautiful painting by Duccio showing Christ leading the souls out of Hades, and this scene formed part of a number of medieval mystery plays, for instance, *The Wakefield Pageant of the Harrowing of Hell, or Extraction of Souls from Hell,* as well as in the Chester and Coventry cycles and in the Easter Play from Redentin.

Since Christ's deed, the state of the souls in death is very different, and to read the description of the death of many of the saints is to have an impression of the light and joy which can accompany Christian dying. Read, for instance, the account of the death of St Columba as described by his disciple and biographer, Adamnan:

And the Saint, his soul not yet departing, with open eyes upturned, looked round about on either side with wonderful cheerfulness and joy of countenance on seeing the holy Angels coming to meet him And after this, signifying his holy benediction, breathed forth his spirit. And it having left the tabernacle of the body, the face remained so ruddy

and wonderfully gladdened by the vision of the
Angels that it seemed not to be that of one dead,
but of one living and sleeping.

Of course, we have not all the spiritual stature and
quality of St Columba and may not have the same degree
of experience of the light-filled world of spirit when we
die, but in principle it is the kind of experience which is
possible for all if who die since the deed of Christ. And if
we have felt the Christ in us during our life, we shall also
feel his accompanying us at the gate of death. If we in life
learn to 'look up,' that is to turn our thoughts to the
things of the spirit, to read, meditate, pray and worship,
then we shall find at the gate of death that 'the stone has
been rolled away' and the angels of the Lord await us.

So we may learn to 'die in Christ' if we have become
convinced through life that we are 'born from God.' In
the words of Rudolf Steiner:

> It is tragic destiny if, in this earthly life, a man does
> not find the Christ, who can lead him through the
> death that stands at the end of life's way, and
> through the death in knowledge.
>
> But if we experience the IN CHRISTO MORIMUR
> — In Christ we die — then, too, we are aware of
> what is seeking to come near us through his guid-
> ance. We feel how the living Spirit arises again and
> out of all things, even within this earthly life. We
> feel ourselves alive again, even within this life on
> Earth, and we see that, through the gate of death,
> the Christ will lead us into Life beyond.
>
> We know now why Christ sent us the Holy
> Spirit, for, with Christ as our guide, we can unite
> ourselves to the Holy Spirit while still on earth.

If we let Christ become our leader, we may surely say, 'We die in Christ,' when we pass through the gate of Death. (*The Mystery of Golgotha,* lecture of August 27, 1922.)

Thus the curse in Genesis: 'Dying thou shalt die' is revoked and the Christian may with confidence proclaim: 'Dying thou shalt live!'

We have journeyed in the course of this book down into the valleys of loss and helplessness. We are aware that for many people of our time death is experienced as a dreadful finality, as an end. For those left behind the passing of a loved one can be felt as a tragic abyss with no future perspective, and we are all challenged to accept that our loved-one has physically gone for good. It is also understandable to feel initially that a great divide separates us from the world of the so-called dead.

We have also tried, though, to show that there is not only a very real link between the living and dead but also a possibility to get to know this world better. At the frontiers of human consciousness we may seek and meet those who now live without their physical bodies. They are profoundly present waiting for us to communicate with them. With Christ as our guide we may cross safely into this world and may for moments experience and commune with those who have passed on. The future of life on Earth will depend a great deal upon us overcoming this separation. Together with them we can move forward and with the help of the angelic world fulfil the ultimate goal of earthly evolution, to create a new Earth and a new heaven and to become truly christened human beings.

Bibliography

Books by Rudolf Steiner:

Knowledge of the Higher Worlds and its Attainment, Steiner Press, London 1976

Occult Science — an Outline, Steiner Press, London 1969, (especially Chapter 3).

Theosophy, Steiner Press, London 1973.

Lectures by Rudolf Steiner:

Ascension and Pentecost, Anthroposophical Publishing, London 1958.

Cosmic and Human Metamorphoses, Anthroposophical Publishing, London 1926.

The Dead are with Us, Steiner Press, London 1973.

'The Ego-Consciousness and the so-called Dead,' *Anthroposophical News Sheet,* Vol.8, 13–16.

The Inner Nature of Man and Life Between Death and New Birth, Anthroposophical Publishing, London 1959.

Man's Life on Earth and in the Spiritual World, Anthroposophical Publishing, London 1952.

The Mystery of Golgotha, Steiner Press, London, and Anthroposophic Press, New York 1940.

Supersensible Man, Anthroposophical Publishing, London 1961.

Theosophy of the Rosicrucians, Steiner Press, London 1966, (especially lectures 3–6).

Other books:

Anon., *The Bridge over the River,* Anthroposophic Press, New York.

Capel, E. F., *Seven Sacraments in The Christian Community,* Floris Books, Edinburgh 1981.

Frieling, Rudolf, *Christianity and Reincarnation,* Floris Books, Edinburgh 1977.

Frieling, Rudolf, *Hidden Treasures in the Psalms,* Christian Community, London 1954.

Jones, Michael (ed.), *Prayers and Graces,* Floris Books, Edinburgh 1987.

Kolisko, E., *Reincarnation and other Essays,* Kolisko Archive, Bournemouth 1978.

Kübler-Ross, Elisabeth, *On Death and Dying,* Routledge 1973. Reprinted Scriber 1997.

—, *The Wheel of Life: A Memoir of Living and Dying,* Touchstone Books 1998.

Lorimer, David (ed.) *Thinking beyond the Brain,* Floris Books, Edinburgh 2001.

Martin, Eva, *The Ring of Return,* Philip Allan, London 1927.

Moody, Raymond, *Life after Life,* Bantam 1976.

—, *Reflections on Life after Life,* Bantam 1978.

Ritchie, George, *Return from Tomorrow,* Kingsway, Eastbourne 1978.

Rittelmeyer, Friedrich, *Reincarnation,* Floris Books, Edinburgh 1988.

—, *Rudolf Steiner Enters my Life,* Floris Books, Edinburgh 1982.

Shepherd, A. P., *Rudolf Steiner: A Scientist of the Invisible,* Floris Books, Edinburgh 1983.

Smythe, Frank, *The Spirit of the Hills,* Hodder & Stoughton, London.

Weatherhead, L.D. *The Case for Reincarnation,* Private publication 1957.